TREASURES

from the
Meher Baba Journals

TREASURES

from the
Meher Baba Journals

1938-1942

Compiled and Edited by
Jane Barry Haynes

Sheriar Press

Foreword

As the pages of this book reveal, it was love that drew Meher Baba's early disciples to him and it was for the sake of love that they remained with him. Today, it is still love that draws those who seek him. This is as he would have it; for Meher Baba's only message has always been of Divine love. His is a message given not in words but through an awakening of the heart.

The story of this extraordinary man is thus a story of love. For while there are many who speak of Divine love, Meher Baba lived it. His life was a life of such love, purity and service that it will stand for all time as the divinely human example of life as it should be lived. To those who have witnessed the simple beauty of his ways, he is the Ancient One: the One who comes age after age to reveal the love of God in the world.

Meher Baba was born Merwan Sheriar Irani on February 25, 1894, in Poona, India.* His parents were Persian, and his father, Sheriar Irani, was known as a true seeker of God. Though Merwan was much loved and respected as a youth, there is little about his early life that indicates his spiritual destiny. He attended a Christian high school and then Deccan College, both in Poona. At age nineteen the veil was shattered and Merwan came to realize who he was.

---

*For a full account of Meher Baba's life see *The God-Man* by C.B. Purdom.

The unveiling began one day in January of 1913 when Merwan, while cycling home from college, encountered an ancient Muslim woman known as Hazrat Babajan. She was reputed to be a Perfect Master, one who had achieved God-realization. From the moment of his first contact with Babajan, Merwan's life changed completely. He began to know his true identity as being one with God. Merwan was then led to contact four other Perfect Masters, each of whom played a significant role in the process of unveiling. One of these Masters, Upasni Maharaj, worked with Merwan over a period of seven years. Finally in 1921, Upasni folded his hands before Merwan saying, "You are the Avatar, I salute you." Merwan began his work as the Avatar of the Age.

Who is the Avatar? At critical junctures in human history, Meher Baba has explained, God becomes man. Though the titles may be many (Avatar, Christ, Messiah), the message of Divine love is eternally the same. In his compassion, the Avatar invariably takes on himself the suffering of the world, and in so doing brings about the spiritual rebirth of humanity. In light of this, Meher Baba has affirmed all the great religions as revelations of God, for it was the same Ancient One who inspired each of them.

In the nineteen twenties "Mastery in Servitude" quickly became the theme of Merwan's life. Tirelessly he and his disciples served the poor, the sick, the outcasts, and the mentally disturbed— establishing schools, hospitals, and ashrams for this work. Then and throughout his life the Master personally cared for those in need. He washed the feet of lepers and bowed down to them saying, "I bow down to the God in each one of you." He cleaned the latrines of the untouchables and worked to end the caste system. Not surprisingly, Merwan

Irani's early disciples began to call him "Meher Baba," which means "Compassionate Father."

During this period of intense activity, on July 10, 1925, Meher Baba began his silence; he would not utter a word for the next forty-four years. There have been enough words given, he said, it is now time to live them. Even in silence Baba continued to communicate on many levels; his warmth and ever-present humor remained undiminished. When he wished to use words he spelled out what he wanted to convey by means of a wooden board with the letters of the alphabet printed on it. Many of his sayings and discourses, including the material collected in this book, were given by this method. After 1954, Baba gave up the board and relied on hand gestures alone.

Meher Baba always stressed that he began his silence in order to break it. By choosing to speak from silence, he speaks the Word of God in our time. This Word is an inner Word heard only in the depths of our being. As Baba himself expressed it:

"External silence helps the inner silence and only in internal silence is Baba found; in profound inner silence. I am never silent. I speak eternally. The voice that is heard deep within the soul is my voice."

This, then, is the spiritual revolution Meher Baba came to bring: the awakening of Divine love within each individual.

Six years after Meher Baba began his silence he traveled to the West for the first time. There he contacted his earliest Western disciples, some of whom were eventually allowed to return with him to India for training in the spiritual life. Many of their experiences are recorded in the articles contained in this book. Through them we are given an immediate and intimate view of life with the God-Man.

Also discussed in this volume is another

significant dimension of Meher Baba's life: his work with the God-intoxicated individuals known as masts. There are, according to Baba, many different types of masts, but in general they may be defined as spiritually advanced individuals whose love for God is so intense that they often appear insane to most observers. In fact, Baba has explained, they are not insane; they simply refuse to adjust to the world, lost as they are in their longing for God.*

Although we cannot fathom the exact nature of Meher Baba's inner work with the masts, we do know that he gave them spiritual help. Beyond this, he indicated that he inwardly channeled their love for God into directions which have benefited the entire world. Baba undertook long and arduous journeys to contact masts and others with whom he had special work. The statistics alone are staggering: from 1937 to 1946, the years of his most extensive mast tours in India, Baba personally worked with more than 20,000 masts, seekers of God, and with the poor in journeys totaling over 75,000 miles.

Meher Baba's mission as the Avatar entered into an important phase in 1949. Dispersing his ashrams and giving up all possessions in India held in his name,† Baba set out on what he called the "New Life." He made the startling announcement that during this New Life he would cease to be the spiritual Master in order to assume the role of a seeker of God. A small number of companions were chosen to accompany Baba and together they set out to live a life of "helplessness and hopelessness."

*Dr. William Donkin gives a complete account of Meher Baba's work with the masts in his excellent book *The Wayfarers*.

†Meher Baba kept only the small plot of land on Meherabad Hill (near Ahmednagar, India) which he had long before designated as the resting place for his physical body when he laid it aside. Today Meher Baba's Tomb at Meherabad is a place of pilgrimage for people from all over the world.

Living fully in the present, without certainty of shelter or food, the New Life companions gave up everything to trust solely in the mercy of God.

Though the full meaning of the New Life is still unfolding today, at least this much may be said: In the New Life God became fully human, forging in human consciousness a new path to himself. The New Life is a life in the world, yet free from the world, in which the seeker loves God for the sake of love alone. In becoming the companion and the seeker, Baba brought into being a new way of seeing and living for all in the years to come who would have the courage to follow.

In his life, Meher Baba had now expressed his full Divinity and his full humanity. In 1952 he emerged from the New Life to declare publicly that he was the God-Man, the Avatar of the Age. For the next seventeen years Baba gave of himself to an unprecedented degree as he moved toward the completion of his work. Baba forewarned his disciples that this work would require of him great suffering, including the shedding of his blood on American and Indian soil. Outwardly, the suffering took the form of two car "accidents," the first in the United States (1952) and the second in India (1956). In one the entire left side of his body was injured, and in the other the entire right side was severely damaged.

In spite of his suffering, Meher Baba opened the gates of his love by giving darshan (personal blessing) to thousands of people during the nineteen fifties and early sixties. During this time he made three visits to Meher Spiritual Center in the United States, which he called his home in the West. One of his last darshans, the East-West Gathering held in Poona, India, in 1962, symbolizes the awakening of oneness through love which he came to bring about. People of many races, nations, and religions came together as one family in the presence of Divine love, and Meher Baba told the gathering what he now tells us all: **"May my love make you feel one day that God is in everyone."**

Meher Baba spent his last years in seclusion, finishing his universal work. The strain of his work in seclusion took a tremendous toll on his health. Nevertheless, Baba was pleased with the results, saying: **"My work is done. It is completed one hundred percent to my satisfaction."** Shortly thereafter, on January 31, 1969, Meher Baba laid aside his physical body to live forever in the hearts of those who come to experience his love.

As we turn now to the beautiful portrait of Meher Baba drawn from the pages of the *Meher Baba Journals*, we should keep in mind that the story of Meher Baba the Awakener has not ended; it has only just begun. Now is the time of the manifestation of his love. He will not speak through a new creed or dogma, for he has not come to establish a new religion. He will speak his Word of love, as he always has, directly to the heart. And in his speaking, the world will once again be awakened to the reality of Divine love in our midst.

Charles Haynes

Meher Spiritual Center
Myrtle Beach, S.C.
June 1979

Preface

It is with much happiness that I see the publishing of
Treasures from the Meher Baba Journals. The material
appearing in this book is brought to the general
public for the first time. The *Meher Baba Journals* were
first printed in 1938 through 1942 for the followers
of Meher Baba. They were not made available to the
public, although certain selections from the *Journals*
have appeared in other publications. Now with this
book a great wealth of original material is brought
together in one cohesive work, thus being made
available not only to the general reader but also to
the vast numbers of new followers of Avatar Meher
Baba who have not had the opportunity to read the
original *Meher Baba Journals.* There is a need now for
this early material which this work responds to, and
in time all of the *Journals* will be reprinted.

Although all of Meher Baba's work is done only
by Him, He uses an instrument to do His work. His
instrument in bringing this book to the hearts of
humanity is one of His Western disciples, Jane Barry
Haynes. With the guidance of Elizabeth Patterson,
the original Editor of the *Journals,* Jane has
painstakingly worked with the voluminous material
contained in the four volumes of the *Journals.* The
goal was to compile and to edit all material
containing Meher Baba's words. *Treasures* includes
informal discourses, sayings, statements and
directives by Meher Baba that have not appeared
before. Other articles and excerpts of articles by

disciples were selected because they contain words of Meher Baba.

The original Discourses of Meher Baba first appeared in the *Journals*. They were later published in India in five volumes and subsequently in England and in America.

The main purpose of this book is to bring together the treasure of thoughts and expressions of Meher Baba as given directly by Him to His early disciples, as well as presenting a vivid picture of the atmosphere existing during the years 1938 through 1942 as recorded by these early Westerners. Their comments take us back in time to their personal experiences with the Master and the priceless training they were privileged to receive from Him.

How great are the pronouncements and words given by Avatar Meher Baba, who is God in human form? Words are words, after all. Just so many combinations of letters are possible in any language. What makes the discourses appearing in this book so significant is the fact that these are the words God has given to reveal Himself and His work to mankind.

Behind the pronouncements of Meher Baba is the presence of the divinity and infinity of God. Beautiful words have been written before, but not until the advent of Avatar Meher Baba have the expressions of God been made directly available to the hearts of humanity in English in an undiluted form. These pronouncements come to the reader not diluted by translation upon translation; they were given directly in the English language to His disciples and printed at His behest.

Scholars have for centuries argued over the accuracy of the Bible; the *Bhagavad Gita* has undergone many interpretations; likewise has the Koran appeared in conflicting interpretations. The message of the God-Man, the Avatar, in the form of Zoroaster, Rama, Krishna, Abraham, Buddha, Jesus and Mohammed have all come to modern man much abridged with claims and counter claims of what He, the Avatar, actually said and did. This is one of the reasons Meher Baba came once again as the Avatar, to reveal in modern language to modern man the Truth of God.

I was personally with Him when much of the material in this book was given by Him. These truths sprang spontaneously, effortlessly, from the depths of His being, as water wells up out of a fountain. The statements of Meher Baba are the revelation of His knowledge.

A word is the clothing of thought and thought is the exposition of experience. All that Meher Baba expressed through thoughts and words is the exposition of His direct experience and carries the fragrance of His love and blessings. Whoever reads it is doubly blessed—by the understanding of what he reads and much more substantially by the sweetness of His love and the conviction of His strength.

When one enters a room full of roses, even if one's mind is so involved with other things that it doesn't become aware of the fragrance, still that fragrance is absorbed by one's senses. That aroma clings to one's garments, to one's person. Likewise the benefit of Meher Baba's words, coming into the consciousness of man where there is no adequate appreciation or understanding, may not immediately manifest; but His words will dive deep into his being, enlightening him when he may least expect it.

As one becomes more acquainted with the discourses of Meher Baba, one gets the feeling of familiarity, the feeling that what Meher Baba conveys is not new, but the expression of deep knowledge felt but never brought to one's consciousness before. The reason for this, my friend, is that Meher Baba is none other than your own real conscious Self, and His pronouncements are the manifestations of your own inner being.

Through His discourses Meher Baba is expressing the highest aspect of your own real being. These words are what your conscious self is expressing to your unconscious self to awaken you to your Real Self.

May His grace be upon you as you read *Treasures from the Meher Baba Journals*. May His words flower into your mind, reaching your heart to awaken the real treasure within your own being.

Ahmednagar, India
November 1978

Adi K. Irani

Acknowledgments

We want to express appreciation to Peggy Stephens for her invaluable help with the manuscript: corrections in the fourth draft and proofreading of the completed work.

All photographs used in *Treasures from the Meher Baba Journals*, with three exceptions, were taken by Elizabeth Patterson and are used with her kind permission. The photographs on pages 24, 84, and 104 were taken by Rano Gayley.

Cover design by Sheila Krynski.

The Editor

"Let these words be inscribed in your heart:
Nothing is real but God.
Nothing matters but love for God."

Meher Baba

MEHER BABA JOURNAL

A MONTHLY PUBLICATION

Elizabeth C. Patterson, *Managing Editor and Publisher*

for the "Meher Editorial Committee"
"Meherabad", Ahmednagar, India

MEHER EDITORIAL COMMITTEE

C. V. Sampath Aiyangar,
(Late of Madras Judicial Service)
Dr. Abdul Ghani Munsiff,
Princess Norina Matchabelli,
Adi K. Irani,
Elizabeth C. Patterson,
Estelle Gayley,
F. H. Dadachanji,
Abdul Kareem Abdulla.

The original members of the editorial committee of the "Meher Baba Journal" appear above.

Contents

Photographs appear on pages *iv,* 2, 18, 24, 29, 30, 38, 41, 46, 48, 52, 84, 93, 94, 96, 104, 112, 127, 131, 140, 141, 145, 172, 177, 180, 200, 211, 241.

Section One

Follow Love

Excerpt from
Lectures Delivered in Mysore

Sayings of Meher Baba

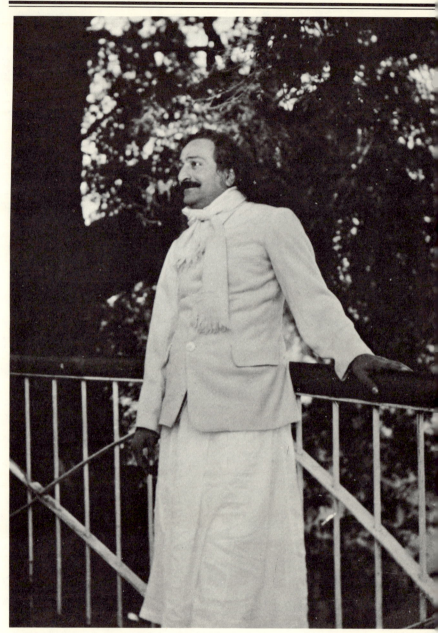

Meher Baba in Ceylon, 1938.

Follow Love

by Elizabeth Patterson

Love is as you experience it. Love varies in degree, and the ultimate final state is union with God.

Meher Baba in His "Sayings" has stated: **"True love means the dedication of one's self or the complete surrender of one's self to the Beloved. It seeks the happiness of the Beloved without the least thought of obtaining happiness from the Beloved."**

There is little question that most of us desire love for the sake of our own happiness, at least indirectly. Yet we might pause to consider that our fountains of inspiration—the great love poems of the ages, the great music which throughout all time has inspired love, the rare expressions in art that have stimulated the heart of multitudes—would in most instances never have been created if the artists had fulfilled their own earthly happiness. The background of the artist's life is usually one of unsatisfied longing. It is the very difficulty of the attainment of true love that, like the ever receding "Holy Grail," lures the soul from profound depths to ever greater heights. The heart that love has carved deep can contain greater and greater love. The bliss of God is a state beyond the dual action of experiencing love, for it is its very Source. The final state has been intimated by Christ in His words: "I and My Father are one."

Love often stirs the heart through a little thing in life, and at the same time has the possibility to end with the greatest thing in life. As much as we all desire love, it is rare to find one soul who dares even the thought of its ultimate completion, rising above all duality and play of opposites to become truly One through God-realization. The personification of Divine Love on earth is the God-Man, who is Love, Lover and the Beloved.

Mystics of all faiths in every land have sought God with intensity of longing. Fervor is invariably a quality of these lovers of God. Rare souls among them who arrived at sainthood, that beatific stage where God is seen face to face, have left to mankind a rich heritage of inspiration and experience which was their inner life. Churches or mosques or temples have claimed their remains after they passed away, and canonized them within the fold, though during their lifetime these ardent, unbounded saints rarely fitted into the pattern of creeds. Mostly they lived apart and sought God through intimate experience of Divine Love which overflowed into their everyday living, and which could not be circumscribed by convention or formalism. They wanted God more than man. They wanted God more than their very lives. They sought and found Him through various paths; but the blessed experience of Divine Love was the same.

If it chanced that these saints possessed the spirit of evangelism, their very fervor and extremity of vision drove more people from them than ever were turned into followers during their earthly life. Of St. Francis of Assisi, we are told that his love embraced all creatures; and one day when the human listeners turned away from his sermon, leaving him all alone, he preached to the birds of the air and these sensitive feathered creatures were irresistibly drawn to him. Even of Christ, the Master, we are told by St. John: "Many therefore of His disciples, when they had heard, said, 'This is a hard saying; who can hear it?' From that time many of His

disciples went back and walked with Him no more."
The greatest of iconoclasts were never the
heretics of the accepted order; they were such as
Christ, Krishna, Buddha, Zoroaster, Mohammed; and
they functioned within the religion of their
respective birth. From them dates the passing of the
old order. The message of love proves ever the great
emancipator. New religions arose only after these
great living exponents of their own teachings had
departed from earthly existence. Even scriptures
were set down oftentimes by disciples after the
Master's mission was finished on earth. No external
religious form took place during their lifetime. Their
own spiritually perfect being was the very temple of
God.

From time to time in the history of religions
there have been revivals when man asserted his right
to know God for himself and demanded his own
experience uncircumscribed by rites and creeds. No
amount of persecution could dim such fervor, and
only when the experience ceased to be direct and
intimate did the wave subside.

Religion itself is inspired from the living example
on earth of God as man. God the abstract can be
worshipped from afar, prayed to, meditated or
pondered upon; but when Divine Love awakens
the heart the affections become concentrated and
objectified. God the Beloved has ever appeared in the
form of a Savior. He who, like Christ, has become
one with God is God-Man.

Every religion has its man who is not only of
God, but is God. To the believers He is the true
manifestation of God on earth. Despite the insistence
on their own avataric manifestation, these great
religions all foretell the return to earth of God as
man. The "second coming" is a part of every faith,
even the more primitive ones. Many Christians today

are given reason to think that St. Mark's prediction is near its time of fulfillment. "But in those days . . . after the tribulation . . . then shall they see the Son of man."

How can we recognize the true Messiah? This has been many times asked of Meher Baba. In a series entitled Questions and Answers, Meher Baba has replied: **"The feeling and inspiration for things sublime, and Divine Love, are imparted by a real Messiah to anyone who comes in contact with Him. A false Messiah cannot do this. Through His Divinity the true Messiah gradually attracts the world to Himself, and the people come to know and feel that He is real. The knowledge and feeling of confidence in His words and works grow gradually into certainty, and masses follow Him drawn by an irresistible force. A mirage attracts the thirsty, but soon it is discovered to be an illusion and not the life-giving water. A false Messiah may attract the attention of the people through outward appearances, by force of personality, or by intellectual dissertations about spirituality; but he cannot do that which the true Messiah can do, i.e., arouse the highest ideals in men and touch the hearts of millions."**

Should we be among those seekers of Truth who look for, or accept, a new manifestation of the Divine One on earth? How best can we receive and serve Him? Following the path of Divine Love has ever been advocated in scriptures. The way has been expressed by Christ in the words: "A new commandment I give unto you, that ye love one another, as I loved you." The Master drew mankind through His personal example of all-compassionate Love, yet He did not make it easy to follow Him. He enjoined those who would follow to "leave all." Christ said: "He that loveth father or mother more than Me is not worthy of Me; and he that loveth son or daughter more than Me is not worthy of Me. And he that taketh not his cross and followeth after Me is not worthy of Me."

To follow a Master has ever required complete detachment. Many centuries before Christ, Krishna said words to this effect: "One who is never affected by circumstance, one who is calm in all trials, who no one else's moods or behavior upsets, one whose faith is never shaken, one who is cheerful even in the jaws of death—such a one only is worthy of loving Me."

An ancient tale which illustrates love for the Master as the way of attainment has been related by Meher Baba: **"In Rama's time a yogi once did penance for one hundred years. There was another man who loved the Master. He did no penance, no fasting. He only loved Rama. One day the Master went walking in the jungle. The first yogi opened his eyes and said to him, 'Oh, Rama, when will I see your formless face?' Rama replied, 'In fifty years.' The yogi was frightfully disappointed and said, 'I made penance for one hundred years and I suffered much, and still fifty years to wait!'**

"The next day the Master accosted the happy devotee, and this loving one asked, 'Oh, Rama, when will I see your formless state?' Rama replied, "After fifty more lives.' The devotee said, 'So soon!' And thereupon he got into such an ecstasy that he died; and as he was dying he saw Rama's formless state." Concluding, Baba added: **"Love is the very essence of Godhood."**

Meher Baba has declared: **"The highest state cannot be explained or expressed in words; thought cannot grasp it; the mind cannot know it. It is the state of the soul beyond the mind—it can be understood only when experienced. I can make you experience it by making you realize it."**

MEHER BABA JOURNAL
November 1939

Excerpt from "Lectures Delivered in Mysore and Bangalore"

by Princess Norina Matchabelli

Meher Baba says, **"I have come not to teach but to awaken."** By the Divine Love that flows continuously through Him, He transforms the consciousness of the individuals who come to Him for liberation, that they may know through experience what the philosophers of all times have tried through theory to teach. Only the Ancient One, who is the veritable incarnation of Love Divine, can awaken in the individual the fire of love that consumes in its flames the lesser desires of mind, body and world, all of which must be relinquished before we can attain Perfection.

Meher Baba says: **"The highest human love is not the highest absolute love. Divine Love is the highest aspect of all-pervading love. One who gets this love gets God. Divine Love is beyond reason and intellect. Nobody can create this highest aspect of love in himself. Divine Love is given and not created. It is grace from the God-Man.**

"It is the real side of religion and the only element which reveals or unfolds the emotionality of the spiritual path. The highest love is the one which is perfectly selfless and disinterested, devoid of all desires and expectations. It is fire—an infinite fire in itself and those who burn in it get purified.

"Philosophies and intellectual gymnastics make one intellectually certain about the existence of God; but it is only the love for God, Divine Love, that

enables one to find Him, to feel Him and to become one with Him."

We must first fall in love with God, then will we be given to love man; that is, "to love one another." This is indeed the highest demonstration of the fulfillment of the divine theme. Meher Baba makes us realize the truth. He makes us realize Oneness in manyness. He makes us realize that spirit and matter, spiritual life and material life, go hand in hand. He says: **"When head and heart, intellect and feeling are equally developed and balanced, then the apparent antithesis is resolved into one divine consciousness."**

Meher Baba has not come to make man different, but to draw man back to the divine source. Through His example, He will help man to find real happiness and liberation within, free from prejudices and unattached to life and its play through opposites.

SAYINGS
OF MEHER BABA

The highest divine knowledge is attained through love (which has in it the spiritual faculties of intuition and inspiration and which is opposed to the intellectual faculty). It is love that makes one transcend the dominion of intellect and gain the state of complete self-annihilation. It is this state that ends in union with God.

There is greater value in conquering the heart of a single enemy than in gaining victory over the bodies of thousands of enemies. The mind is capable of turning the bitterest enemy into the sweetest friend by constantly thinking well (charitably) of him.

Love resembles death in that it annihilates snobbery, vulgarity and all distinctions.

Forgetfulness of the world makes one a yogi; forgetfulness of the next world (heaven and hell) makes one a saint; forgetfulness of God means Realization and forgetfulness of forgetfulness is Perfection.

Divine Love causes its captive to forget his own individual existence by making him feel less and less bound by the trammels of human limitations on his onward march, till he reaches a point where he can raise himself to the realization of the highest in himself.

The trinkets of this world cannot tempt the true Divine Lover. He does not feel the appetites and cannot enjoy sound sleep. He resembles a fish just taken out of water. He is restless until he is united with the Beloved.

To understand man completely is to understand the whole universe in all its variegated multiplicity.

Jealousy is not born of love, but of petty-mindedness, and dies simultaneously with the death of petty-mindedness.

Do not be afraid of God, for how can you love Him if you fear Him? Fear and love do not go hand in hand. The truly religious man is he who is God-loving and not God-fearing.

Though the heart cannot take the place of the head nor the head of the heart, they are not necessarily enemies of each other. Intellect counts for very little in the spiritual life. When the heart and the head are equally developed and balanced, one's progress on the path is more rapid.

To realize the Supreme Being as your own Self is to realize truth. The universe is the outcome of imagination. Then why try to acquire knowledge of the imaginative universe instead of plumbing the depths of your real Self?

Whereas atheism is generally born of intellectual vanity, agnosticism is often the outcome of intellectual humility. Humble, honest agnosticism will eventually be converted into a firm conviction of the reality of God.

True knowledge is that knowledge which makes man, after Self-realization, or union with God, assert that his real Self is in everything and everybody.

True bhakti (worship or devotion) does not necessarily mean the observance of religious rites and the muttering of mantras or bhantras. But it certainly means the continual repetition of any one name of God, or the continuous thinking and remembrance of God.

When in you the limited 'I' disappears, the infinite 'I' in you manifests itself automatically.

That is real service where there is no thought of self at all.

Selfless service may not only bring you to the foot of that mystical mountain whose summit is Self-realization, but it may enable you to climb far on the path. Finally, it may bring you in contact with a Perfect Master and cause you to surrender to Him.

True selfless service means the rendering of service to others without any thought of gain or reward, and also without the least intention of putting others under an obligation.

Though millions say that there is nothing but God, to most men this gross world is all in all and God is unreal or a phantom.

Upon the altar of humility we must offer our prayers to God. Humility is spiritually of greater worth than devotion. It is easier to be devout than to be humble, but devotion in many instances proves to be a stepping-stone to humility.

Real happiness lies in oneness; wherever there is duality there is trouble.

Revenge follows hatred and forgiveness follows love. Without love none can cultivate the noble habit of forgetting and forgiving. You forgive a wrong done to you in the same measure in which you love the wrongdoer.

You can counteract a disease only by its antidote. Love is the antidote to hatred. When you feel like hating a man try to remind yourself that he is a form of your own Self.

Jesus taught what religion is: to find God within . . . through love. And that is the message of the Master to this age and it is the meaning of His life.

Section Two

Accounts by Those
Who Follow the Master

News About the Master

by F.H. Dadachanji

Meher Baba's Work in the West

The greatest reformers of life throughout all time have tried to bring about the blending of East and West to create a family of humanity. The new man will be understanding in his acceptance of the differences of traditions and conceptions of life, exchanging the modern mental culture of the West with the true spiritual life of the East.

After fifteen years of strenuous work in India preparing His Eastern group of disciples, Meher Baba came for the first time to the West in 1931. He laid the foundation of the new phase of His work when He gathered around Him an intimate group of Western disciples and planted the seed of spirituality in the lives of hundreds whom he contacted in Europe and the United States. In His own words: **"I have come not to teach but to awaken."** Meher Baba thus qualified His spiritual mission in the world. In fact, He has come to awaken in the heart of man the true experience of spirituality.

The West Is Brought to the East

In 1937, after years of longing and severe tests for the Western disciples, the Master drew a group of about twenty of them to India where they resided at "The Meher Retreat" in Nasik, which had been specially established for them.

In a discourse to the group in Nasik, Meher Baba explained the meaning and purpose of this particular phase of His spiritual training as follows: "The infinite embraces all expressions of life. Spirituality does not need renunciation of worldly activities. It means the internal renunciation of mundane desires. Mere asceticism does not lead to spirituality. Perfection cannot be perfection if it shrinks from the dual expressions of nature and tries to escape from entanglements. It must assert its dominion over all illusions, however attractive and however powerful. A perfect being functions with complete detachment in the midst of the most intensive activity and in contact with all forms of life. Divinity includes all that is beautiful and gracious. Every one of you has to help in My work according to your individual capacity; and you have to be in touch with the world in accordance with the work that lies in store for you. I will teach you how to move in the world, yet be at all times in inward communion with Me as the Infinite Being. You will have to experience both the comforts of Nasik and the discomforts of Meherabad* and be detached from each."

The Western men and women who came to Nasik were individuals of different nations and religions; people whose ties of life have the same weight that all ties in life have; who have professions and duties; who, leaving behind their families, unconditionally accepted Meher Baba's school of life-spiritual that is based on experience and practice of the divine theme. Meher Baba teaches without intellectual method. He awakens in the heart of man the innate divine being that reveals spiritual virtues which man has to practice in life: unselfconscious goodness, selfless service and love impersonal.

*Meher Baba's colony near Ahmednagar

Meher Baba at Nasik, February 18, 1937, with (left to right) Delia deLeon, Nadine Tolstoy, Margaret Craske and Norina Matchabelli.

The fruits of this ideal training will be known to the world one day when these sincere seekers will fully mature in spirituality and return to work in different spheres of activities in the world, participating in the Master's mission for the spiritual upliftment of humanity.

After eight months of personal training at Nasik, Meher Baba dissolved the group, sending them back into ordinary life to put into practice that which was revealed to them.

The East Goes to the West

In August 1937, Meher Baba renewed this phase of exchanging East and West, but *vice versa,* by bringing His close group of specially trained Eastern disciples for a visit to the Western group in Europe. His Western disciples prepared for His coming, and selected as a central location an international place— Cannes, France.

A remarkable peculiarity of Baba's method of working is the fact that wherever He moves He takes with Him His spiritual "baggage," which does not consist of possessions but of disciples—those working elements who are trained to live everywhere, in all situations, as impersonal mediums of His directing will. One unusual member of the group was Mohammed, the "God-mad man." This man, whose spiritual advancement is exceptional, is the principal resident of the "Mad Ashram" in Meherabad. The Master has kept him near wherever He moves, and so he was also taken to Cannes.

Furthermore, it may be noted that the small group of Eastern women who accompanied Meher Baba to the West have, for over six years, lived a life of strictest discipline in absolute seclusion. For years they have neither seen men nor heard their voices; they have not walked beyond the boundaries of the Ashram-on-the-Hill. They have been kept aloof and away from Baba's external activities. These women, although modern in culture and customs as individuals, have unconditionally accepted for years the severe training of humility, doing any kind of manual work, and have passed through severe tests which one would hardly believe human nature could endure. It may also be explained that this special training is the reverse of the life of His men mandali, who practice in the outer world what might be termed herculean tasks. The interesting fact is that this seclusion for the Eastern women was maintained in the strictest manner throughout the voyage and also during their stay in the West at Cannes, despite the innumerable difficulties caused by the inevitable formalities of travel and other complications arising from many circumstances.

After the Master's return from Europe in November 1937, He resided at Meherabad with His intimate groups. Three of His Western disciples who came with him joined the Eastern group of women in the Ashram-on-the-Hill. Two more arrived in February from America. The rest of the group, the men mandali, as usual stayed in the old quarters below, along the road. Not far from there, behind the well, is the special place reserved in the ashram for the "God-mad" men.

Many hundreds among Meher Baba's followers and admirers came throughout the year to Meherabad for the darshan of their beloved Master and to keep alive the close contact.

Meher Baba's 44th Birthday

Meher Baba's 44th Birthday was celebrated this year on the 18th of February at Meherabad, and there was a large gathering of several hundred who came from all over India. One feature of this year's celebration was a separate arrangement whereby the secluded group of ladies celebrated for the first time the "Love feast" in their own quarters on the Hill, together with the many women who came from afar. Arrangements were made for a hundred of these women guests to stay for three days on the Hill.

The general public celebrated the Birthday in the mandali quarters below. The Westerners, together with the Eastern women guests, participated in both these celebrations. The entire function was characteristic in its cosmopolitan atmosphere and observance devoid of ceremonial formalities; spontaneous and rare in expression of true Love between the Master and His devotees; forming a bond so close that one can only qualify it as that of a beloved Father with His children.

This experience, destined only for those who enter into the spirit of pure love and devotion, has remained ever unforgettable. Living proof of Meher Baba's compassion was the feeding of the five thousand poor and destitute, and also the distribution of *ladus* (sweets) to all with His own hands. From sunrise to sunset a stream of humanity, needful in body and soul, was drawn to receive His prasad, or gift with a blessing.

The Shift to Panchgani

In the middle of March 1938, Meher Baba transferred His quarters temporarily from Meherabad to Panchgani for the summer season until the middle of June. This hill station is about 5,000 feet above sea level, sixty miles from Poona. It has a very cool and bracing climate even during the summer. It was partly for the Westerners who have been staying with Him and particularly for the work that He wanted to do there that this shift to Panchgani was arranged. The tropical heat of Meherabad during the summer would have been unbearable for the Westerners and might have created physical complications detrimental to the spiritual progress which is the prime objective of their coming to India to live with Meher Baba.

The main object of Baba's visit and stay in Panchgani was, as usual for His work, mostly *internal*, difficult to grasp with our limited minds. A large bungalow was hired for the season on a very secluded hillside just on the edge of Tiger Valley. Here all the ladies of the group, Eastern as well as Western, stayed together.

None of the male members, as usual, was allowed access even to its precinct. Half a dozen members of the mandali stayed in a small outbuilding to look after the necessary arrangements for the daily life of the group and to attend to the routine work, consisting mainly of the extensive communication kept up regularly with the numerous devotees living in India and abroad.

After allotting comfortable rooms and space to everybody in the main bungalow, Baba selected for Himself the storeroom attached to a kitchen, apparently unused for a long time and actually in a state of ruin, with very low ceiling and no opening except a cracked wooden door. But this soon was transformed into a spotless cabin for His use. A small annex was reserved for the "God-mad" man Mohammed.

In years past Meher Baba had come to Panchgani. In 1930 He stayed there in grass huts with His mandali of over twenty men for about two months. During this period He had a special cave carved out and constructed overlooking famous Tiger Valley. Here He Himself retired in seclusion and here He also kept half a dozen of His disciples in retirement and seclusion with Him in the vicinity of the cave in small huts. All were fasting, living only on milk. Simultaneously He kept seven others of His disciples in seclusion at different places in Meherabad. Many others as well, living in the outside world, volunteered to fast with the Master, partaking only of milk for forty days.

After His own retirement in seclusion, Baba sent some of His intimate disciples to stay in His cave for different periods ranging from forty days to six months, fasting, at times on milk and on special occasions living only on water, for forty days. This cave ever since has been a holy place of pilgrimage for those who hold such abodes of spiritual masters as sacred. Even those who come to this hill-station for a holiday and visit this cave wonder how in this spot, haunted by panthers and leopards (for which the valley is a playground), one could retire in seclusion and stay alone during the dark nights without firearms or even a lamp. Except for the few people who live in the small village far down in the valley, no one would venture to be in the surroundings after dusk.

Two of Baba's Western disciples also have recently stayed in this cave for short periods—an American disciple, Garrett Fort, the well-known scenario writer from Hollywood, in March 1937; and this summer an American disciple, Elizabeth C. Patterson. An extract of her experience follows.

An Experience in a Cave Overhanging Tiger Valley

"In all earnestness I asked Baba if I might spend a night in the cave; and He promised me, yes, but that He would set the time. Weeks later, I reminded Him and He only smiled: **'Do you wish to go now, or wait until it is the right time?'**

"At last one day, the sixth of May 1938, He told me that I should go to the cave and remain for exactly twelve hours. Baba and the lady disciples accompanied me to the cave on this spiritual adventure; and at 6 p.m. exactly Baba locked me in, giving me the key inside. The last thing that I remembered, before everyone left me shut in alone for the night, was Baba's hand extended through the iron bars, resting upon my head as if in blessing.

"The moment after they had all disappeared around the bend of the path there was profound stillness. Fleeting thoughts passed through my mind, but these I controlled, as Baba had instructed me that I should concentrate throughout the night and not sleep, unless I could not keep my eyes open any longer. According to Baba's instructions, I lit a lantern exactly at ten minutes before seven and then lay down.

"Once I heard heavy thuds, like steps, approaching on the path and I waited anxiously for someone to appear; but the sound, although close, passed away and probably was a cow or a buffalo which had been grazing on the mountainside. Four

Meher Baba with Elizabeth Patterson at the cave at Tiger Valley in Panchgani.

stars in the shape of a kite, which resembled the Southern Cross, stood out in the sky more vividly than the rest. I remember looking at my watch to find it was not far from midnight. Determined to remain awake, I continued to think of Meher Baba.

"Unexpectedly a shock, like electricity, passed through my body from head to foot; I felt it particularly along the spine. It continued in waves of varying currents and became so strong two or three times that it seemed to lift me—as would a rush of wind. Soon I felt myself swinging into space, the bedding unevenly swaying beneath me. I felt that if only I could remain on it, as on a 'magic carpet,' I would be carried safely; but it rocked so much that I then remembered to call out Baba's Name and immediately the 'troubled waters' were stilled. Coming out of a kind of daze, I found my arms folded across me, as they cross the arms of the dead, and they were so numb that it took a while before I could move them. Whatever the state was which I passed through, I was *consciously unconscious* during it.

"A seeming sense of time passed when I was aroused by the cheery sound of voices, which I recognized to be those of my friends. They apparently were inside the cavern and called to me that it was five o'clock and that they had been sent to summon me. I remembered Baba telling me not to leave the cave until 6:00 a.m. sharp, and this seemed conflicting. As I was wondering what to do, the thought came to me that I had better do what Baba Himself had told me. At that moment Baba glimmeringly *appeared* in the entrance and light flooded the cave with unusual brightness. He smilingly answered my mental inquiry by saying: '**Do as I said; leave only at six.**'

"Some hours later, opening my eyes and looking at my watch, I found it was nearing six o'clock and I rose to leave the cave. I felt fresh and invigorated—

daylight was faintly penetrating the cave.

"After returning home to the bungalow I asked Baba: 'Was it symbolic?'

"Baba answered **'Yes. In the future you will know in detail its full meaning.'** "

The Return Home

In the middle of June Meher Baba returned from Panchgani to Ahmednagar with the group and stayed in a bungalow in the Cantonment area till the end of August, since the ashram quarters on the Hill at Meherabad were undergoing changes and extensions to make room for the new Westerners and additional Easterners to come.

Meher Baba and His group left Ahmednagar on the 25th of August 1938 to take residence at Meherabad, where He has remained since.

Come and See
Part I
by Kitty L. Davy

*For as the lightning cometh out of the
east and shineth unto the west, so shall
the coming of the Son of man be.*

"Come and see the Acropolis at Athens," writes
one enthusiast to his friend at home. "Come and see
the Ellora Caves," writes another; "to see these alone
is worth a trip to India." "Come and see the famous
masterpieces in Florence; their beauty will leave a
lasting impression," writes a third.

Many there are ever ready to spend their
savings, their earnings, their fortunes on these
different quests; but how few are ever prepared to
spend time or money on the Quest of the Spirit
which seeks for the perfection of beauty that is
manifested in the human-divine form—the vision of
Divine Love. The present generation is seeking, but
is nevertheless skeptical. It fears disappointment and
disillusionment. It does not accept the Quest of the
Spirit as the Great Adventure that holds out to those
who accept its challenge a cross as well as a crown,
danger as well as safety; for the sign-post of this
Quest says: "He that loseth not his life for My sake
has no part in Me." Man wants security in the
spiritual realm as he now seeks it in the material. So
the spirit groaneth within until such time as God
sees man's willingness to cooperate, and he is born
anew.

Said One long ago, "Come and see," in answer to
His disciples' question, "Where dwellest Thou?" They

came, they followed, they forsook all and found the "pearl of great price."

Today, nearly 2000 years later, this same Voice spoke to a little group in answer to the same question, saying: "Come and see." They obeyed and are here—a small group gathered from all parts of the world; not in Nazareth, but in a spot not very different—Meherabad—situated on a hill looking down upon the village of Arangaon to the south and to the north Ahmednagar, the famous military fort of past days. A group not unlike that early group of men and women of passion; impulsive, of little understanding. Some like wavering Peter, some like doubting Thomas, some with the intuition of John, some with the weakness but the supreme love and faith of Mary Magdalene; some filled with the cares of the household like Martha, some like Mary—calm and never ruffled, looking up at her Master with eyes that tell how she understands, ever ready to respond to His mood, ever thoughtful of His human needs and not worrying Him with her little cares and troubles after a weary day's work. How Jesus must have loved that thoughtfulness for His human side, for we know that He was indeed tired at times.

Today can be observed a scene not unlike that of 2000 years ago. Meher Baba, our beloved Master, coming up the hill in the midday tropical sun and, before He has had time to enter His room, being beseiged by one wanting a letter to be signed, another with some petty grievance, another with some domestic matter of no importance; and Meher Baba patiently listening, not turning away, weary and tired though He be after bathing and feeding the God-mad down below.

Previous to Meher Baba's ashram in Meherabad there existed but a stretch of land between Ahmednagar and Arangaon, a distance of about six

Top photos: Meher Baba at doorstep of cabin on Meherabad Hill, 1935; Meher Baba in "old building," Lower Meherabad, 1935. Lower photo: Meher Retreat on Meherabad Hill, 1938, with kitchen quarters visible in background.

Mehera Irani, Meher Baba's closest woman disciple, with her favorite dog Kippy at Agra, 1939.

miles. Twenty years ago Baba "pitched His tent" a mile outside this village of Arangaon, giving the place the name "Meherabad," which means Land of Mercy, Kindness and Prosperity. The surrounding land His followers tilled and sowed. Later was built a dispensary to which the poor from the neighboring villages come for free treatment and a hospital for the mad who today would be called the "psychological mad," those sensitive types, restless within with their longing for God and who without a guide have got lost on the Path, losing their mental balance and appearing outwardly as though mad.

Alongside is Baba's own dwelling, a small room built of red brick with a green tiled slanting roof. A little beyond are the quarters for His men disciples. Then across the railway track and up the hill are the women's quarters, above which can be seen for miles around the dazzling white tower, with its ever-burning light a beacon to all, a red and white flag flying from its flag-post—the Eastern symbol telling those who pass by, "Here dwells the Blessed One." Nearer can be seen, written in large golden letters: "Mastery in Servitude," Baba's motto for all who follow Him.

Up on the hill live the women from the West, sharing now in closest detail the life of the Eastern group, who have been here since its foundation. The youngest member of the group is Meher Baba's own sister, Mani. All live an active and busy life, secluded only in the sense that—except for the Master—no men enter the precincts. Outside the boundary wall is the women's hospital, a few steps only from the sacred spot where Meher Baba has gone into seclusion for months at a time, and which previously was the site of the Prem Ashram.

Such are the surroundings of Meher Baba's earthly spiritual home, the atmosphere of which is beyond comparison. One speaks from experience, having only recently returned from a six months tour of India, visiting during that period the recognized spiritual places, and returning to this place—set on a holy hill—to breathe again with joy inexpressible the pureness of its air, the freshness of its breezes and the beauty of Divine Love and Peace woven into every grain of its soil. This is Meherabad, the radiating center of all Meher Baba's activities; the place of pilgrimage for the future.

What have we seen? One, like Jesus, who draws followers to Him through love. One who says: **"I have only love to give and all I want is love."** One who does not promise His followers earthly happiness, but who says nevertheless, **"Be happy, be cheerful. Do not worry, do not brood."** Thus teaching from the very beginning that self-mastery holds the golden key to Divine Perfection.

Picture Meher Baba with His group of men and women disciples and without even the spoken word noting their every frown, every anxiety, every thought and feeling, and perhaps in front of all or taking one aside, spelling out on his board (His self-chosen means of communication): **"What is wrong? What has upset you? Are you worrying about anything?"** There stands the Silent One alongside you with His Infinite Love and Knowledge, helping to bring to the surface and to have spoken out all the pent-up feelings, many of which are sanskaras from the past as well as the present, some of which you are not even conscious of. And saying at the end: **"Will you promise Me one thing? You say you love Me. You say you want to please Me and to see Me happy. Then remember, be happy and do not worry. I will help you. I know all. I know how deep is your love. Just do as I say. Love Me, and leave the rest to Me."**

So the atmosphere changes from darkness to light, and each feels that here at last is One who understands, One who loves; and simultaneously the highest aspect of love is revealed. The almost impossible task of not worrying, done for the sake of pleasing Him whom you love, becomes your dearest task, although demanding herculean effort.

Such is a true picture of our beloved Master, Meher Baba, truly the Christ carrying out His work for the saving of mankind; the supreme example of divine sacrifice, loving all equally and serving all equally, who, though possessing everything and wanting nothing, yet stands out amongst us as both the Lord and Servant of all. Why? Because He loves; His sacrifice is for love, with no other purpose or concern connected with it. This is Truth. Sacrifice for love alone.

Come and see! You will not go away empty, if your search for Truth and Love is sincere. Meher Baba will "quicken the Spirit within" and Divine Love once awakened will not slumber eternally, even though dimmed at times. God longs to realize Himself in us infinitely more than we can long for Him. The strength of the ocean will always be greater than that of its separate drop, and when once you face this Ocean of Love, like the needle before the magnet, nothing can resist its drawing power. Meher Baba is the Ocean, having become one with it, and we are its individual drops, individual souls of the One Soul, separated but temporarily, that God might realize Himself consciously in us through Love.

How do you know that Meher Baba is the Perfect One? This is the natural question. Is it through faith, through love, through intuition or through knowledge? By knowledge? *No.* Only God can know God. There can be but one reply. By Divine Grace, by the Will of God which awakens the spark of Divine Love. Even so, this glimpse into Divine Knowledge must be upheld by the response of our love and faith, and the latter being, in the words of the Apostle, "the substance of things hoped for, the evidence of things not seen" has in it an element that may both fail and err. But Divine Love from the heart, though weak at times, because not perfect in manifestation as yet, cannot err. Hence Meher Baba says, **"Love and love Me always more and more."** Divine Love can never be mistaken for carnal or human love. This is the verdict of those who have experienced both.

To us who follow Him, Meher Baba is Love and Truth—the most perfect of all human beings. Perfect in love, in wisdom and understanding— attributes of God Himself. Said the Avatar two thousand years ago: "Be ye therefore perfect, even as your Father which is in heaven is perfect." And again: "The disciple is not above his master; but every one that is perfect shall be as his master," reiterating the Truth taught by Krishna and by all the Avatars: that all is God, in God and potentially God. To realize consciously this oneness, through purity of Divine Perfection, is the purpose and the goal of life.

This truth Meher Baba has come to reiterate and to make live again. Towards this Perfection He will lead the world and those who follow Him, that all may be as He is; that they may know and experience consciously through Divine Knowledge their oneness with God.

Come and See
Part II
by Kitty L. Davy

Come and see and bear witness to Meher Baba's
perfect knowledge and understanding of all human
beings. The Divine Psychologist using Divine Love as
His medium of working; see how patiently He works.
As there can be no perfect knowing of the True
while the false ego obliterates the real "I," He must
lead you towards understanding this false ego which
exists only in this world of duality. It is this
awakening which gives you freedom — freedom
from bindings of convention, bindings of fear,
bindings that limit and bindings that inhibit. From all
these He will set you free, that the Spirit within may
shine forth undimmed. How? By making you
conscious first of its nature, and then at every
opportunity giving it knock after knock, till you can
remain calm in the midst of all, and the false ego
thus starved loses its energy until it ceases to exist.

Meher Baba with His Infinite Knowledge leads
you to the point where you have to face up to the
truth of yourself. There is no escape in a life lived in
a group, living at close quarters under one roof,
bound in by four walls. Every detail of the life of
each is known to the Master. For example: someone
insults you, calls you names—calls you a liar.
Immediately your ego is hurt. You boil inside, and if
this resentment is not controlled, it shows itself in
anger and excitement. In this way you feed the ego,
and instead of decreasing, it increases. Meher Baba,
who sees all, calls both parties together. He rebukes,
He scolds for this lack of control and lack of love,
saying: **"If you cannot love each other, and it appears**

that you cannot, then take practical steps to see that you do not fight and can give in to one another. When you begin to feed the ego with the help of the mind and you feel resentment and excitement approaching, start laughing, start dancing, go outside for a moment until the mind is under control. But control at all costs."

How slow all are to learn this lesson of control! No wonder the Master asks for implicit obedience. He knows that without this order, the struggle would be a hundred times greater. It acts as a reminder. It focuses our thoughts on Him and not on our actions. But the closing of the scene makes even the rebuke worthwhile. Baba, looking up and smiling, says: "Now go; forget about it and do not brood. Throw it all over. It no longer exists. Be happy, be cheerful. This is my order." (He knows how difficult it is for us to forget.)

Thus we experience Divine forgiveness that truly forgives and forgets. Meher Baba may withhold the fulfillment of certain statements He may make until His own time; but if He says that He forgives and forgets, you have abundant proof that this is so. He trusts you as before.

There are few things that Meher Baba really dislikes, but one of these is excessive remorse and tears. If He orders you to forget and to stop brooding, you must obey and control the mind. It is lack of control that prevents your doing so. Hence Baba's insistence on obedience, which is always to help you and for the sake of the work. Says Meher Baba: "If you cannot be cheerful and obey when I tell you, then why stay near Me? You sacrifice all— your home—your friends—your freedom—for the bindings of four walls, and all this for love; yet you spoil what would be a perfect sacrifice by this absolutely disastrous lack of control."

Yet another example: You have come to Baba never having experienced what it is, say, to feel jealous. Circumstances have been such that you have had no cause to be jealous. Baba, knowing the very depths and thoughts of each, sees there the seed of jealousy—a past sanskara—waiting but for its opportunity for expression or sublimation. He also knows that while it remains dormant, there can be no freedom from its binding effect.

What does He do? He does two things. He uses Maya to overcome Maya, and at the same time sublimates its energy for His own work. How? He knows you love Him. He knows you want to express that love in working for Him. He knows you want His love. For a time He will give you a great deal of attention, giving you many opportunities of serving Him. Then begins Baba's game. He appears to pay more attention to others, to be unconscious of your presence. He sends others on errands you have hitherto done, and gives work to another that you had begun to look on as your special job. He remarks nothing, apparently ignorant of all; then suddenly He looks up at you and says? **"What is wrong? What has upset you? Aren't you well?"** You answer: "I do not know." Baba suggests any number of causes for your change of mood, and leaves you no peace until the truth is out, and you realize that perhaps it is jealousy.

Jealousy of what? You want to do everything for the Beloved. The restless enthusiasm for the moment blinds you, and the loving thought escapes you that it is more beautiful to stand by and let others who love their Master equally with you, and who want to serve Him, have their share—yes, and yours too. How happy is the Master, for His work is done. Now it is up to you to do the rest. You must go on loving more and more, but learn to control this natural

Kitty Davy feeds Jumpoo the monkey at Meherabad, 1938.

feeling of jealousy (natural because our love is not perfect).

We cannot grasp that with God all are one, and that "they also serve who only stand and wait." To control the outward expression of this jealousy is now your task, even if it still tortures the mind; and from now on it will torture like hot burning coals. Baba will give you abundant opportunity to prove your efforts in this direction. He will test you almost to the breaking point until you have gained mastery over it.

But better it is, says Meher Baba, to have these difficulties to overcome than to have nothing to control. They serve their purpose towards self-control. Is not this in itself a message of hope? Human nature changes but little until the last stage of the journey is reached. It is the control over lust, greed and anger that makes us different from the animal, and it is this control that Baba asks of all who would follow Him.

Meher Baba seldom praises. **"Let your reward be that whatever you do is done to please Me."** But should He for a special reason want to show His appreciation, then He shows it; not by the spoken or spelt-out word, but silently, with a look so expressive, so full of love, that the effect of it is infinitely more lasting than any words could be.

The path towards Perfection along which Meher Baba leads His followers is fourfold. Selfless action—love and devotion—mind control and knowledge through experience—combined with complete surrenderance to the One you follow as your Master. Baba says what all the Avatars before Him have said: "He that forsaketh not all that he hath, he cannot be my disciple." Only when you have given up everything—body, mind and wealth—for the sake of love, can you know God.

To follow Meher Baba as your Master and yet to want material security for the future has no meaning. He must be your security both now and for all times. To those who have given all He says: **"You have given all for love. All Mine is yours. You are My own and I will look after all who are Mine."**

No less important on the road to Perfection is non-attachment to the success or failure of all action. Let all you do be to help. Says Baba: **"If it be your duty to kill a dog to save three cats, let your thought be that of helping the cats. Have no attachment to the action of killing."** And: **"Be attached to neither violence nor non-violence. Fight if fight you must, but let your motive be to help."** And: **"Eat to serve your God, but not for the pleasure of eating. So only can you learn freedom from all desire and be attached only to love."**

"Let thy concern be the action and never the gain it may yield," says the *Bhagavad Gita*. This alone will give you the poise and balanced mind to which neither rebuke nor blame can cause any mental disturbance or bring up any anger or resentment.

"Think always of me," says Meher Baba, **"whatever you may be doing, and gradually it will be I doing everything through you. 'I' the doer— not you; so what concern have you with the result?"**

Meher Baba has been known to root up what has taken months to build. He started His Ashram for the God-mad at Rahuri, and when at its zenith He saw those working there becoming attached to the success of it all—200 patients coming daily to the out-department—He tore the whole structure down in three days and transported the mad by bus to new quarters here. Meher Baba builds and destroys, but all for a purpose. At every point He must test those who come to Him.

We now come to the Truth underlying all Meher Baba's workings: that God alone is real, so Love only is real. Love is what Baba first awakens and it is what He emphasizes continually. He asks nothing of you until you love; and the love that He awakened in this writer eight years ago, after only three days contact with Him at His retreat in Devonshire, has never been quenched. It was as if a dam burst and the years of longing for goodness, truth and beauty were at last satisfied.

It takes One who is Divine Love to awaken Divine Love. As each fresh cycle approaches and human nature becomes more receptive, fresh and

Meher Baba in the doorway of Rahuri Cabin, 1938.

higher glimpses into Divine Love are given by the Avatars to the world. Christ taught that love of your neighbor is second only to love of God. May it be that the Avatar of today, Meher Baba, when He manifests His true being to the world, will have even a deeper meaning to give to the concept of Divine Love. One thing is certain: God's Love is not perfectly understood by man. We cannot have perfect knowledge of Divine Love until our knowledge is perfect; so the Avatar will always be misunderstood.

How does Meher Baba want you to express your love? In selfless service done cheerfully and happily. This is His first and last order. Selfless service in all external actions as well as selfless service in internal actions. This is spiritual renunciation. It is continual, unceasing, this struggle for self-mastery, the road to perfect knowledge leading to perfect service.

"It is through work," says Meher Baba, **"that you come to purity. Work dedicated to God frees you from responsibility and binding, and by so doing you surrender to Him whom you serve for love. This leads automatically to love for all whom you serve; because how can you hurt one whom your Master loves without hurting Him—your Beloved; and how please Him whom you love except by pleasing those whom He loves equally with you? Love will take you still further, for would you wound your Beloved if, by so doing, you caused another standing by, whose love may be deeper than yours, to suffer?"**

"Love suffereth long and is kind" says the writer addressing the Corinthians. No phrase expresses more beautifully and more perfectly our beloved Master, Meher Baba. He once said: **"Do you know how I suffer from you all not understanding Me and My love?"** How many of us say to the Master, "Give me God-realization. Give me union, and I will give you all I have. I want nothing else, and then I will serve you to the very end." What a crucifixion! What a sword thrust into the very heart of the Beloved to condition thus God's Love. Better that we bury our heads in the dust at the Master's feet. Let us rather be as the great Saint Rama Goa of South India who used to cry: "Oh God! Let me remain Thy lover forever. I do not want union, for then I cannot love You." But says Baba: **"The result of this love is union. Love must naturally long for union, but it must be ever ready to give up the longing for union if it be the wish of the Beloved, and not think of self at all."**

The nearest approach to complete Oneness and affinity with the Master is when He allows us to experience something of His infinite suffering—an experience known only to the lover and His Beloved. Love longs for this supreme privilege, a longing deeper than that for service, but it is not to be had for the asking!

The Avatar must suffer. Will it be that history will repeat itself, and those to deny Him, when the time comes, will be His own countrymen?

This is an attempt to draw truthfully and simply a picture of what all will witness if they obey the call of the Master: "Come and See." This is life. This is the truth lived in close contact with the Master. He becomes your conscience, and from this there is no escape—no relaxation. Your life is keyed up to its highest note—a note your Master pitches for you and which you must ever try to sound with the helping hand and all-seeing eye of Him who walks ever with you: Meher Baba—the Truth behind all and in all.

Ramon Lull in his *Song of the Lover and the Beloved* writes: " 'What is love?' said the Beloved. 'It is that in which I die daily, and which is all my will.' "

Excerpt from "Meher Baba's Tour of Nine Days Through Central India"
Part I

by Princess Norina Matchabelli

In October 1937, while still in Europe, Meher Baba called me and said: **"We shall return soon to India, and there I want you to join Me on a trip through certain cities. I want you to see Me at work there as you have seen Me at work here."**

When Meher Baba says to do a thing, that is the moment when He wants it done; and when He wants it to be done, that is the time to do it. So now that we are in India He has drawn out the following itinerary of this nine-day trip on the west coast and through Central India:

We are to leave Meherabad on December 20th, 1937, and we stop at Talegaon, Bombay, Navsari and Nagpur, returning to Meherabad December 30th.

. . . We leave Meherabad at 6:00 a.m. precisely. The sun is quietly rising behind the distant hills of Chandbibi, where lived the daring Mohammedan queen in the past history of Ahmednagar.

Our road leads via Poona. We motor along the soft curving mountains I know so well that encircle the distant horizon of Meherabad and which we contemplate every evening in Baba's company at sunset. The atmosphere is still and blue at this early hour, and everything seems to function right in its own experience. We pass white bundled figures herding goats and lazy dogs abandoned in their own struggle for life, lying around within the boundaries of a tiny village. Baba, looking at all these desolate lives in poor huts, says: **"How I love all these."**

We approach Poona. In the distance we recognize the landmark of the white-towered Turf Club with its elegant gates, and we all express the wish to see Baba's childhood home. Baba willingly accepts the plan.

It is 8:00 a.m. when the car gently swings into a small lane and stops in front of a large comfortable-looking house. Adi, Baba's brother, accustomed to surprises, hears the familiar sound of the horn and walks out leisurely to greet us, holding in his deep emotion. Humbly he prostrates himself to the ground and takes darshan from his unique Brother.

Meher Baba's mother, greeting us cordially from behind a curtain, apologizes for not being dressed for the occasion. But Baba, who times with a measure unfathomable, does not wait. He rushes us out of the main house over to the other side of the lane where, at the joining point of three streets, stands a smaller house—Baba's childhood home. The house apparently is not in use, although the windows and the shutters seem to be newly painted blue. With great animation Baba Himself opens the door. The inside is empty, the atmosphere clear, quiet and awesome. There are two rooms on the ground floor. To one side of the entrance is a circular wall forming a bathing space where "little Merwan" used to be given his ablutions, thus the mother who meanwhile has arrived tells us.

Meher Baba makes the following statement: **"One day men from all parts of the world will come here on pilgrimage."**

A small vertical stepladder leads to the upper floor. Baba shows us the way; we follow and stand in a chamber-like space, crushed under its low ceiling. Here Baba used to spend those significant hours in anguish, waiting to descend to make Himself available to mankind as the Pure Human, as the divine experiment in its fulfilled order in Being, in

Shirinmai, Meher Baba's mother, at "Pumpkin House,"
Meher Baba's birthplace, Poona, India.

Truth. Here He remained aloof in His divine selfless
state, still unselfconscious—and sometimes disturbed
by good friends and members of the family,
especially by His good mother who did not trust His
unfathomable state and wanted to keep Him the
same as He was before: Merwan, her precious son.
Doing her best to hold Him down, closer to her, she
tried to make him eat specially well prepared food.
Baba, in a wistful, joking manner, wanting to make
us acquainted with the facts, describes how He used
to hide the food, which was too heavy for Him to
digest. He would put it into a drawer in the room
and then into His pocket at nighttime, when He
would leave the house and deposit it somewhere in
the street for hungry dogs to eat.

Overwhelmed by the atmosphere of many sacred

memories, we are carried away . . . feeling the conscious contact with Him present; He the Life, the God-realized Man. The divine theme seems incredibly vast against the background of small facts. With a sudden changing of mood, Baba bids us quickly climb down and return to the main house.

Baba takes us through all the rooms which at present are occupied by His mother, Shirinmai; Adi, His younger brother; and His brother Behram's family. The house is comfortable and roomy and neatly kept.

Baba wants to show us more. We rush on to the courtyard. There is the famous well with its excellent water and the big tree that Baba recognizes as an old friend. The connecting smaller houses encircle this garden, and at present are occupied by strangers who all are very well acquainted with the sacredness of the place. At the other end Baba points to two doors carefully locked with huge chains and padlocks. His mother, who is anxious to dramatize the past of her dear son, says, "This was His prayer-chapel." But Baba, discreet as usual, explains: **"Here I have spent many hours in solitude, and in that room** [pointing to the other door] **Gustadji** [then His colleague, now His disciple] **kept vigil."**

We return to the main quarters; but before leaving the house, Baba pauses at the doorway. He seems to be absorbed in His childhood memories and suddenly says, **"Here, when I was a small boy, I used to play wild games with my chums."** Think of those small fellows who, then in no way conscious of His Unfathomable Being, casually touched Him in their boyish manner and enjoyed in furious adversity their childish games. But how He loved them! At that time Merwan was full of fun and mischief, but also knowing and wise; His word even then was accepted. People around used to listen to the charm of His voice with its incomparable sweetness. The unfathomable life in Him drew from the Divine Source and created the thrill of indivisible Love, unselfish affection and friendship in so many hearts.

Baba's arrival and departure is always quick, but profound in its effect. We are ordered to leave, and without special ceremony we wave goodbye through the window of the car and speed off to Talegaon, our next halt.

Meher Baba with Princess Norina Matchabelli.

Excerpt from "Meher Baba's Tour of Nine Days Through Central India"
Part II

by Princess Norina Matchabelli

We speed on to Bombay. It is the twenty-first of December. The air is nice and cool; quiet and blue is the range of romantic mountains where Shivaji, the king and great warrior, destroyed the Mohammedan enemies who fought against him.

In Bombay, Meher Baba is given quarters in the home of a close disciple on Frere Road. Many people are already waiting in the long corridor when Baba begins to open the eternal well of His great curing Life.

Later on, while discussing among ourselves some subtle subjects, suddenly Meher Baba with the speed of lightning interrupts the wasted exertion of our minds, making the following statement on selfless service:

"God as God alone is not consciously man, and man as man alone is not consciously God. The God-Man is consciously both God and man; so the God-Man is both Lord and the servant of the universe. Lord, in the state of helping all souls toward reality. Servant, as continuously bearing the burden of all. To serve Him who serves all is serving the universe.

"Selfless service and love are twin divine qualities. Only the one who loves can serve.

"Serve your Beloved God-Man and you are serving your own self in every other self.

"The service He exacts is for your own spiritual benefit; but this service must be spontaneous, willing, wholehearted, unconditional and not expecting any reward. This service is an ordeal which tries body, mind and spirit; or else wherein would the perfection of serving lie if it were to be easy and at one's convenience? The body suffers, mind is tormented, but the spirit of the selfless server of the Master experiences the bliss of satisfaction.

"Only the one who has can renounce. A king giving up everything and becoming a beggar exhibits true renunciation; and so only the one who, without any question and regardless of consequences, serves the God-Man really serves; otherwise it would be just like paid labor."

Meher Baba and Healing

by Countess Nadine Tolstoy

Since I have met Meher Baba, all my existence, with all life's common and uncommon interests and activities, joys and sorrows, has received a new perspective and significance. It became a fascinating fact in view of *one* sure end to achieve.

The contact with the God-realized man became the source of all good and of a new, pure and true vision of life. Standing as a perfect example to follow, Meher Baba guides men with supreme authority and knowledge. He does not make them follow patented courses, artificial and often dangerous practices. He does not promise easy ways for great outcomes. He awakens *within* men the imminent resources that gradually and naturally unfold in the disciple or devotee. The grace of His Love is a profound and pure experience, which convinces without words and sets the awakened soul on the Path.

In this ashram, the Meher Retreat of Meherabad, we witness a microcosm in full function, individually and collectively. Here we see all expressions of human nature, all varieties of work done. On the top of the hill overlooking the wide horizon, in the center of a vast circle of space, stands the new building, interesting in its symbolic simplicity of balance and unity—the Meher Retreat. The high white tower in the center bears the insignia

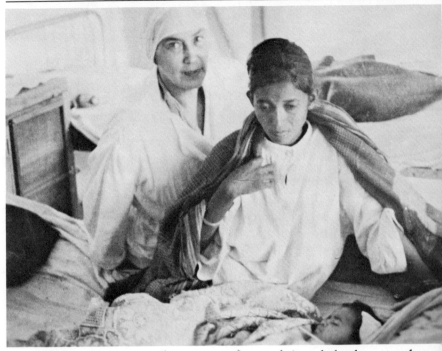

Nadine Tolstoy with young mother and first baby born at the hospital on Meherabad Hill.

of all spirituality—"Mastery in Servitude." Being situated on a hill, it gives a wonderful feeling of floating in vastness of pure sky and space; only the ethereal line of distant mountains on the horizon gently breaks the fascinating monotony of landscape. Right beyond the wall, our ashram has recently expanded into a few additional buildings to suit the extended activities planned by Meher Baba for the group. In this simple, unpretentious building is the Free Hospital for the poor, women and children; right next to it is the office of the new Meher Baba Journal.

Meher Baba has said: **"There are thousands of hospitals in the world; I could have here thousands** of nurses to work. If I have given this work in the hospital to you, it is because I want you to learn serving in real spirit . . . selfless service."

To the hospital came mostly poorest elements of the country, wrapped in their rags and worn-out saris; emaciated and panting, they dragged themselves up the hill. Others were called for in cars or were brought on a stretcher to the door of the hospital. Mostly unwashed and heads uncared for (which one could plainly see and smell), helpless in their ailments, they are the truly destitute. Often they brought their children along, having no one to care for them at home. They were patient and enduring, humble and childlike, and one could not help loving them. These people we had to wash immediately, change into new clothes, put to bed and make them feel at home.

I will always be grateful for the opportunity to contact these simple people. Faith and devotion to our beloved Baba always beautifully shines in their expressive eyes! When Meher Baba came to the hospital, giving an embrace to one, a loving pat to another, touching with His healing hand the ailing body, how quick and sincere was the spontaneous response of the heart. Sick, they dragged their paining limbs to Baba's feet with surrender, asking for His darshan. When the medicines and injections given by the professional doctor could not bring due relief, Baba's appearance and loving embrace acted as the "holy wine," reviving their hopes and giving them the lasting impetus of recovery. The joy of seeing Baba, and the faith that He alone can really help, acted within their hearts as a sure remedy.

The hospital presents a natural medium of spiritual learning. Serving the sick and suffering, one spontaneously is led to self-forgetfulness. The response to Meher Baba's guidance becomes natural and easier. Yet even the portion of unresponse brings greater evidence of the failing of the ego, thus showing the results of the test.

Meher Baba's frequent visits to the hospital have been to all a source of great inspiration, of renewed inner efforts *to be* in order to do well. *To be* is to act quietly; *to be* is the impersonal aloofness and detachment from results of action; *to be* is less self-consciousness in our outer and inner efforts, equally ready to act in spontaneous response to the moment's need.

The act of pure love freely given, disinterested in motive and result, is a pure act; it obliges none and bears no mark of self-satisfaction. The Master's guidance brings it out in the devotees as an inward urge, of its pure volition, constantly purified through His Infinite Being.

As Meher Baba says: **"Do not think that in serving others you put them under obligation to you; be happy that they have given you the opportunity to serve."**

Excerpt from "Who Is That Man?"

by Countess Nadine Tolstoy

Meher Baba's humor and wit is subtle and to the point; He will lift the lower moods in laughter and fun, making everybody light and alert, free from heaviness and limitations of self-consciousness. His greatest words of Truth become alive, sparkling in wit and inspiration. In His subtle way He stirs the joyous qualities in human nature and changes one's moods accordingly. He likes cheerfulness as a sign of real, free response to Him. In all of life, in beauty and humor, in ugliness and misery, in richness or poverty, He is the One in each heart—in joy or sorrow. One moment He works and plays with joy, another moment He works and plays with pain, always turning the game into glimpses of spirituality and greater detachment.

To help the control of the mind He gave a wonderful message about the mastering of disturbing thoughts to someone in a desperate state of mind: **"As long as you do not interpret thoughts into actions you get the opportunity thereby to exercise control."** And further to calm the troubled seeker He says: **"If no thoughts assail you, what is the difference between you and the stone that has no thoughts at all?"** Yet He will show the outlet and the way, saying: **"Cease the mental tension, train your mind to pass over thoughts; don't countenance them until such time that you can surrender the mind itself. When the mind is surrendered, there is no question of happiness or unhappiness. Because of the**

thoughts, the past lives' sansakras are spent away—
they come and go. It is like a wound up alarm clock:
it will ring at the appointed time, but only so long
as the winding is there will it ring and run its
course. But take note not to wind it again by
indulging in action. Still if you want to die, die in
Me, in my Naad, by getting hold of Me firmly. That
is salvation, that is real dying. Worldly dying is not
the thing. Remember that the whole world is a zero.
Mind is the universe, mind is the man, the woman,
the beast.

"Life in the ashram is not only a bed of roses
but of thorns too."

As His work is in life, through life and for life,
as One Life in its ultimate meaning, He links all life
events with their spiritual good. All our inclinations
are used naturally for their perfected expression in a
detached, impersonal, free way. His main concern is
to see that it is done with love, from the *heart*: work,
write, speak, serve from the *heart* . . . and with that *He
awakens Love.*

He makes one rich with love and pure in heart.
He says: "**Love is God—lust is Satan.**" He compares
the lustful man to a cart on one wheel. Disentangling
man's consciousness from bindings, He makes it free.
He says: "**Spiritual freedom ought to be the only
goal of all, for it includes everything else—moral,
mental and material.**

"**Love is the very essence of Godhood. But not
the spider type of love. The spider says, 'Oh fly, for
you I have built this palace, come and become one
with me.' It is the life-giving love I want, not the
life-taking love. All yoga can be done only with
love. But it needs the grace of one who himself has
that Love. Love holds all keys to all mysteries of
life. Love awakens.**"

The fundamental law of being is One for all.

This happy wise Man says: "The self is self's curtain. That is why it is almost impossible to know self. It is so completely one that unless there is duality the experience cannot be had; but when the duality is there then ignorance creeps in. Eyes cannot see themselves unless the mirror reflects them. The sparrow to see itself needs a mirror; but when it sees itself in the mirror, it thinks it is some other sparrow and fights with the reflection. Why? The duality caused by the mirror made the sparrow see itself; but ignorance made it think its own reflection to be another sparrow. Unless there is a mirror the sparrow cannot see itself and when the mirror comes, the ignorance comes too.

"For the soul to know itself, the medium of Maya and its creations is necessary. But Maya and its creations come, ignorance comes too, and instead of knowing itself through Maya it goes on fighting with Maya. Ignorance must go, and soul will know itself."

Meher Baba says: "Material freedom binds you to Maya and leads to spiritual avoidance—it is no freedom. The freedom that helps towards truth and spirituality is real freedom. But some who have faith and believe in God lead a life without character and fail to make any progress; while there are others who do not even believe in God but lead such a noble life that they automatically come closer to God. Whereas atheism is generally born of intellectual vanity, agnosticism may more often than not be the outcome of intellectual humility. Humble, honest agnosticism is sure sooner or later to be converted into firm conviction of the reality of God.

"Uncontrolled mind plays havoc with your soul. My mind is like the ocean: all the filth, all the good and bad is absorbed in it. In a small pool filth upsets the water. In the ocean all is drowned. So is My mind. Your limited mind becomes stagnant with a few bad thoughts. Universal bad thoughts cannot affect My ocean-like mind."

So He serves humanity, continuously bearing its burdens. One can well see in Him that, as He says: "Selfless service and love are the twin divine qualities. Only the one who loves can serve."

One day when His work will be done He will lay aside His body, and then His body will be buried in the place assigned. Millions of pilgrims will be drawn to this Abode of Peace and Love; to this Abode of Rest, of Hope, of unforgettable memory, as a unique place for the comfort of the heart.

Excerpt from
"St. Teresa of Spain"
Adapted by Will Backett (London)

Meher Baba visited Avila, Spain, the birthplace of St. Teresa, in 1933. He had a very special work to do there. He and His disciples all fasted for twenty-four hours and during that time they were not to touch Him. Together they walked over the hills. The next day they saw many of the treasures of the cathedral and were very exalted; the spiritual atmosphere was not unlike that of St. Marks in Venice or that of Assisi.

After visiting the shrine of the Saint, on the site of her former home, they walked to a hill behind the town, looking back at Avila as they climbed up a dusty donkey track—just the same as Teresa had traveled during the thousands of miles she journeyed in Spain. Meher Baba had been there long ago.

They came to a small plain between two rocky summits and strangely shaped boulders. Twenty miles away were the snow-topped peaks of the Sierra Gredos. They reached the special, memorable place, a sandy lonely rock carpeted with thyme, basil and other herbs. Time seemed to roll away and it was wonderful to be with Baba there. The fast was broken on their return.

Meher Baba explained that in Europe, as in other countries, there are saints and advanced souls whom He calls His dear ones; and to manifest externally His expression of love for His dear ones, He abstains from eating when blessing their places. There are many holy places connected with spiritual workings in Europe. The four in Europe—St. Marks in Venice, a place on the Ligurian Coast, Assisi, and Avila—had now all been visited with Baba. Baba arranged that one of the party should visit this spot in ten days, every day for seven days in succession.

. . . In prayer, St. Teresa writes, "the soul is suspended in such a way that it seems utterly beside itself. The *will* loves. The *memory* is, as it were, lost. *Understanding* makes no reflections but is not lost, it is not at work. It is, as it were, amazed."

Memory and reflection being in abeyance, time merges into timelessness, freeing the will entirely to energize the Love Divine, resulting in complete elimination of personal desires in full consecration of the whole nature of God, which the understanding recognizes.

Thus consciousness receives when will, memory and understanding are passive and the soul is upraised.

A Master can expound the laws of the subtle world in which Teresa and the saints and seers move. Meher Baba explains: **"Nature is much bigger than what a man can perceive through the ordinary senses of the body. The hidden aspects of nature consist of finer matter and forces that interpenetrate and exist together with the physical. There is no unbridgeable gulf separating the finer aspects of nature from its gross aspects. The finer aspects of nature are not perceptible to man, but they are nevertheless continuous with the gross aspects. They are not remote, and yet they are inaccessible to his consciousness. This is due to the fact that his consciousness is functioning through the physical senses which are not adapted for perceiving these aspects of nature which are finer than the gross aspects. He is unconscious of these 'inner planes,' just as a dead man is unconscious of sounds; and** naturally he cannot also deal with them consciously. For practical purposes they are other worlds to him.

"The pathway of a man through the divisions of nature's hidden part is called gnosis; the object of the various systems of religious ceremony and doctrine is to prepare for it. Gnosis is the internal but actual pathway inside a human being. Though it is not exactly like a material road, it is distinctly perceptible to the internal eye of a real mystic or gnostic, who actually has the experience of traveling along it."

Excerpt from "Sacred Verse in East and West"

by Will Backett

At Meher Baba's Birthday celebrations at Nasik in 1937, some of His Western devotees were present and heard one of India's great singers improvising for over an hour on this theme to Krishna, in which all hearts there could echo the presence of our beloved Master:

> *O Beloved, go not to Thy great temple at*
> *   Mathura,*
> *Nor to the house of the rich, where are great*
> *   preparations;*
> *But come to the hut of the poor man,*
> *Who has nought to offer but a cup of cold*
> *   water, and the love of his whole heart.*

On another occasion at Meherabad after Meher Baba had been explaining the *Bhagavad Gita* to some of the Western disciples, He gave them the following Western hymn to memorize and added: **"Everything in the Gita is expressed in these few lines by the Western mystic."**

> *Take my life and let it be*
> *Consecrated, Lord, to Thee.*
> *Take my moments and my days,*
> *Let them flow in ceaseless praise.*
>
> *Take my hands and let them move*
> *At the impulse of Thy Love;*
> *Take my feet and let them be*
> *Swift and beautiful for Thee.*

*Take my voice and let me sing
Ever only for my King.
Take my lips and let them be
Filled with messages from Thee.*

*Take my silver and my gold,
Not a mite would I withhold.
Take my intellect and use
Every power as Thou shalt choose.*

*Take my will and make it Thine;
It shall be no longer mine.
Take my heart, it is Thine own,
It shall be Thy royal throne.*

*Take my love, My Lord, I pour
At Thy feet its treasure store.
Take myself, and I will be
Ever, only, all for Thee.**

Such surrender is the object of all worship.
Meher Baba has said: **"Almost the whole of
humanity is concerned with Bhakti Yoga, which in
simple words means the art of worship. But it must
be understood in all its true aspects and not merely
in a narrow and shallow sense in which the word is
commonly used and interpreted. The profound
worship based on the high ideals of philosophy and
spirituality, and prompted by Divine Love, doubtless
constitutes true Bhakti Yoga. Nevertheless it may be
said that the ritualistic worship which the masses of
humanity confuse with religion is Bhakti Yoga in its
incipiency or initial stage.**

**"The average man should follow his creed,
whatever it be, in all sincerity, regardless of rewards
to come and with only the aim and object of: 'I want
nothing but you (God).' But when I speak about
following one's creed I mean that everyone should**

---

*Frances Ridley Havergal, 1874

be free to base his worship on the religious ideals and methods that appeal to him most; and not that one should stop dead at believing or disbelieving in certain statements in a particular scripture about subjects that are generally beyond the sphere of the intellect. It is the act of worship from the heart, and not thoughts and beliefs, that counts in the religious province."

Excerpt from "Wonders in Numbers"

by Will Backett

Some years ago the Master gave the mandali the following explanation to a spiritual riddle:

"Every Sadguru (Perfect Master) is divided into twelve parts, which mean his circle—the circle is invariably of twelve persons only.

"The human body is composed of five elements of nature, viz., air, fire, earth, water and ether.

"Now each of us possesses mind, but so long as the mind controls the body, the perfection state (i.e., of a God-realized person) cannot be reached. If the mind crosses the first and goes into the second plane, the first is realized. When it goes to the third, the second is realized, and so on, until the seventh, when it becomes perfect.

"So the human body, which is composed of five elements of nature, passes through the seven planes (5 plus 7) and becomes a Sadguru, who, as said above, is divided into twelve parts."

Meher Baba has explained that the evolution of mind or thinking appears in the least degree in the stone stage. This latent human form at that stage is, of course, quite imperceptible to the naked eye, being extremely latent, but with eyes, nose, mouth, hands and feet compact in the last degree. Meher Baba says:

"It is like a cloth doll, which can be made to resemble an uneven piece of stone when carefully folded up; and as the stone evolves, these imperceptible compact parts of its body begin getting unfolded. The same process continues in the metal and vegetable kingdoms; as in the tree, the branches crudely represent limbs, and the root, which is underground, the hair on the head. This stage in the tree represents the first of five principle 'turns' of the compact human form from 'stone' to 'man.'

"The second stage in the animal creation is in the worm, where feet lie flat on the ground, with two hands, two feet, twenty fingers, etc., not perceptible in their proper order and very crude and minute.

"The third is in the fish, where the face is upward and the body raised, say, 60 degrees and with compact hands and feet as fins. The last fish form is in the crab, which has connection both with the water and the earth.

"In the fourth stage the waterfowl appears, having connection with both water and air; and the last but one aspect of this stage is the cock, which has little connection with the air, but is almost entirely on the earth. The last form of birds is of a large burly one with a long beak and a lolling piece of flesh on the chin.

"The next 'turn,' the fifth in the animal creation, is in the kangaroo, which through various higher forms, such as the dog and the monkey, culminates in man."

Summarizing these stages, Meher Baba concludes:

"(1) From under the ground to its surface.

(2) From the surface of earth to water.

(3) From the depth of water to water surface.

(4) From the surface of water to air.

(5) From the air to the surface of earth.

"There are distinct stages in the unfoldment of the human embryo before birth that correspond to certain aspects of these 'turns.' On the 'reverse' path of the soul these 'turns' correspond to the superconscious planes of cosmic development, culminating in God-consciousness.

"The evolution of consciousness proceeds side by side with the evolving form of man and reaches the stage of instinct in animals, and intellect in man, becoming inspiration in advanced human beings, and illumination. When all sanskaras are removed, consciousness freed from limitation realizes the Self."

Meher Baba illustrates five different stages of human consciousness in this gradual evolution:

"(1) Ordinary waking state in which the universe is experienced with full consciousness.

(2) Ordinary dream state in which the universe is experienced in a semi-conscious state.

(3) Ordinary sound sleep state in which nothing is experienced.

(4) Divine dream state.

(5) Divine waking state in which one gets the experience pertaining to the Divine. In the first state the soul experiences the universe, and in the last the soul experiences the Self but not the universe."

Meher Baba enumerates seven stages of conscious bliss:

"(1) Throughout the animal kingdom from the fish upwards.

(2) In ordinary human beings.

(3) Yogis in the trance state, awakening kundalini through concentration, passing through the first, second and third cosmic planes of consciousness within the 'subtle' sphere.

(4) On the fifth cosmic plane, in the mental sphere, where one becomes engrossed in the light of the Almighty.

(5) On the sixth cosmic plane.

(6) On the seventh plane of God-realization.
(7) The bliss of sahaj samadhi during the process of 'coming down' from there and after regaining the gross and subtle consciousness."
The Perfect Master retains this perfected consciousness while in the world, in which he also experiences all the five stages of human consciousness. Baba illustrates full consciousness, which the soul develops through the evolution of forms, by comparing it to a flashlight. In the ordinary human being this falls on the gross body, through which the soul can only experience the gross world and remains unconscious of the subtle and mental worlds because the "flashlight" of consciousness is not thrown upon its subtle and mental bodies. At this stage the soul is also completely ignorant about itself. The functioning of the flashlight of consciousness of the ordinary human being is limited to the gross body because of sanskaras; but when they are partly worn out it becomes possible for the soul to withdraw the flashlight of consciousness inward and throw it on the subtle body; while working thus the soul is only conscious of the subtle world.

Consciousness of the mental world is obtained through a similar process of wearing out more sanskaras to enable the flashlight of consciousness to turn onto the mental body, at which stage the soul becomes unconscious of both the gross and subtle worlds, and is centered solely on the mental world. All three worlds are in varying degree shadows of the Oversoul; but since the mental world is closer to Reality than the other two, the soul may now be said to "see" God. However, the soul does not know itself as being One with God, because the flashlight of its consciousness is upon its mental body and not upon itself.

Meher Baba compares man's mind to a cup containing the lusts and ambitions and intellect through which the spirit accumulates impressions of its experiences; and He illustrates the operation of higher consciousness thus:

"Suppose a pilgrim in Egypt reaches the mental sphere and conceives the idea of seeing America. The pilgrim has not even to think about America, but simultaneously with a wish on his part to be there, he will find himself actually there, sooner than the time it takes to think about America in the ordinary way. And why does the pilgrim in the mental sphere travel faster than thought itself? Because he does not, strictly speaking, travel; as the mind is everywhere, the pilgrim in the mental sphere can be anywhere he likes without using his gross and subtle organs. With the disappearance of all sanskaras it becomes possible for the soul to withdraw the flashlight of consciousness from the mental body and turn it towards itself. At this stage the soul is completely unconscious of the universe, since it has dropped all the bodies (gross, subtle and mental) through which alone the universe can be experienced. God-realization is thus a distinct goal for the soul, and every soul is bound to realize its own true state. In God-realization, the knowledge which was latent in the Oversoul (Paramatman) from the very beginning becomes manifest in the full consciousness which the soul has developed.

"Paradoxical as it may seem, upon the false consciousness of the universe—the outcome of sanskaras—depends the real consciousness of the 'One.' The relationship between the 'real' and the 'illusion of reality' may be symbolized by numbers, as '1' and '0,' since 'nothing' is the converse of 'all.' In the number '10,' therefore, we see that '0' receives its value only by being associated with the '1,' and that is the truth behind the 'zero' value of the universe; that it needs to be regarded in its relationship to the one reality, which thereby itself acquires self-knowledge. Thus, God is at the heart of the universe and becomes revealed through its association with Himself. His infinite knowledge, bliss and power are at the back of the mind of a Perfect Master, whereas at the back of the mind of an ordinary person is intellect."

In the foregoing brief summary of evolution of body, mind and universe, the numbers 5 and 7 in the Master's spiritual riddle appear, as well as the number 3, in the threefold nature of man's evolving consciousness through his three "bodies"—physical, subtle and mental. Meher Baba explains that freedom from limitation in God-realization assumes three forms:

(1) Most God-realized souls leave the body at once and forever and remain eternally merged in the unmanifest aspect of God.

(2) Some retain the body for a time, but their consciousness is merged completely in the unmanifest aspect of God.

(3) A few God-realized souls keep the body, yet are conscious of themselves as God in both His unmanifest and His manifest aspects. They know themselves as God in everything, and are therefore able to help everything spiritually and to make other souls realize God.

There is a threefold standpoint in ceremonial religious observance which may become the initial stage of true worship and the highest divine knowledge. This **"comes in and through love"** which, Meher Baba continues, **"has in it the spiritual faculty: intuition, inspiration and illumination. It is love that makes one transcend the dominion of the intellect and gain the state of complete lower self-**

annihilation . . . becoming less and less bound in the onward march by the trammels of human limitations."

Describing the Kasti ceremony of the followers of Zoroaster, Meher Baba says: "The three knots which are tied during this ceremony indicate: (1) good thoughts; (2) good words; (3) good deeds. From the material standpoint the striking off of the sacred thread while reciting the Kasti prayers signifies the removal of the dust that may be on the thread, which is the outward manifestation.

"From the esoteric religious standpoint it signifies the driving away of bad desires and bad thoughts, which is the mental manifestation.

"From the esoteric spiritual standpoint, it signifies the wiping out of sanskaras.

"If it is done in right good earnest and with great sincerity of heart, it certainly wipes out some of one's sanskaras; but if performed a thousand times a day mechanically or for show or for the observance of custom it will be of no avail.

"In the first four cosmic planes, the pilgrim traveling on the path of worship, love and devotion (Bhakti Marga) obtains glimpses of eternal joy, and on the fifth and sixth cosmic planes, which are in the mental sphere, he experiences direct enjoyment of the eternal joy; he only achieves the state of infinite bliss when the seventh and last plane of perfection is reached, in God-realization.

"The pilgrim who travels on the path of service (Karma Marga) obtains glimpses of eternal power on the first four cosmic planes, and becomes a mahatma on the fifth and sixth planes in the mental sphere of cosmic consciousness. The pilgrim on the path of knowledge (Dnyan Marga) has experiences relating to the knowledge aspect of the highest as he passes through the six cosmic planes; and on the seventh realizes, with pilgrims on the former two paths of love and of service, the state of eternal knowledge, bliss and power of the highest.

"A God-realized soul does not become something utterly different from what he was. He remains what he was, and the only difference which the realization makes in him is that whereas he previously did not consciously know his true nature, now he knows it. And he also knows that it has really been what he now knows himself to be: the infinite Oversoul (Paramatman). All that he has been through is just a game; for it is nothing but the process of finding oneself."

Unfoldment of Life

by Will Backett

Meher Baba has described the greatest of all problems as "the problem of self-realization, which includes all the petty problems of the world and humanity put together, that remain unsolved for ages until a Master takes up that mission and helps suffering humanity struggling in the meshes of Maya to be out of it.

"Self-interest, caused by low selfish desire, is the root cause of contemporary world chaos and individual misery.

"My manifestation will embrace the economic, social and religious aspects of life. It will spiritualize all human activities in art, science, music, politics and drama. In the near future a great universal drama will be enacted, the theme of which will be pure love, selfless service. I will play the leading part in this world-awakening drama."

Meher Baba has explained that "the unfoldment of life and consciousness for the whole Avataric cycle, which has been mapped out in the creative world before the Avatar took form, is endorsed and fixed in the formative and material worlds during the Avatar's life on earth."

Excerpt from
"Twenty Years with Meher Baba
. . . Bombay Phase"

by Dr. Abdul Ghani Munsiff

One night while seated alone with Him, I found
Meher Baba in a very communicative mood, and a
little teaser from me brought forth the following
discourse on the subject of Divine Love. Reciting the
Persian couplet:

> "Isha awwal dar dile mashooq paida mishawad ta
> nassozad shama kai parwana shaida
> mishawad.
> (Love originates first in the heart of the Beloved;
> unless the lamp burns, how can the moth go
> mad after it?)"

Meher Baba explained: "It is assumed that there
is a lover and the Beloved and the connecting link
between the two is love. Although God is love
universal, let us for the sake of argument concede
that God at first begins to love or to attract a talib
(aspirant) by means of sufferings. The aspirant, not
understanding the true significance of such an
overture from Him, begins to protest and resist.
This results in easing the situation for the time
being and again a pull is exerted towards the party
to be attracted. The moment that sufficient love is
kindled in the heart of the aspirant, which expresses
itself in the desire for seeing God, He then becomes
indifferent. In this manner the process of attraction
and repulsion continues for an undefined period,

ultimately resulting in the union of the two. This is exactly what Hafiz tries to explain when he says:

'Yak sare mooy ba daste mano yak sar ba doost
Sal ha bar sare in nukta kashadash darma.
(With one end of the string in my hand and the
    other end in the friend's hand,
This tug-of-war has been going on for years on
    this point.)'

"In proportion to the love that may be awakened in you, there will be some moments when you will hate Me also. This hatred or repulsion is the resistance offered by you when I am trying to attract you towards Me by My internal love. In the course of time, you will begin to respond to My love with equal intensity and then the force of My love will relax; i.e., I shall become indifferent. The Master has love for all the members of His circle; and this treasure of Divine Love which has come to Me through Babajan and Maharaj will be shared at its proper time with the members of the circle and others in accordance with their connection, services and sufferings. The esoteric fact which I want you to remember is that the Beloved (God) is more keen and eager to realize the lover (man) than the latter's anxiety and longing for such a union."

Arangaon Dispute

by Elizabeth Patterson

Staying at Meherabad I feel that I live everywhere and nowhere. Yet through Meher Baba, this speck on the map of India which is unknown to the world seems like the pin of the hub that fastens the giant wheel, with its spokes radiating out to the throbbing cities, the arteries of civilization, and to the furthermost ends of the earth.

Colorful local events assume importance which could have their counterpart in other communities of the world, only against different backgrounds.

The little village of Arangaon, with its four hundred inhabitants, is about a quarter mile from Meherabad. We can hear its temple bells from our hilltop. The village had its importance, together with Ahmednagar, in the time of the brave Mohammedan queen, Chandbibi, who lived several hundred years ago in the Mogul period, and who led her armies to victory (although she, riding on her white horse, was killed in the battle). The great picturesque fort in Ahmednagar, which is large enough to house whole barracks of British troops today, was constructed by Chandbibi when Arangaon was a thriving village.

At present in Arangaon there are interesting architectural facades, doorways, windows and other relics of past grandeur, including parts of the old wall. But now the place is crumbling and poor.

There is an ancient feud existing in Arangaon, the true details of which are lost, but which is kept alive in the village through the inhabitants taking sides; two "parties" have long been formed. The village has always been divided against itself, despite the fact that the inhabitants are practically of one caste.

Meher Baba's Birthday or other occasions when the villagers come to see Him, or when they invite Baba to their village for a fete, are the rare occasions when both parties come together peaceably. Recently Baba was invited by the headman of Arangaon, as spokesman, to come to their great fete day and give the villagers darshan, or blessings.

Knowing that His Western disciples had never seen anything of the kind, Baba invited us to accompany Him on what turned out to be a touching miniature "triumphant tour"; for every villager was there, lining the cobblestone streets and throwing flowers before the car in which Baba rode. He smiled upon them as the divine parent, which He is in truth, and we could feel their hearts respond.

The headman of the village, together with musicians and native dancers, slowly walked or danced the half-mile distance from Meherabad to Arangaon with its winding streets. At a place especially prepared for Baba near the ancient gateway on the far side of Arangaon, the villagers each in turn passed in front of Him and, in the manner which is as old as the East itself, prostrated themselves before His feet, and He touched their heads in blessing. *Baba always lets happen that which is prompted by the human heart.*

It happened a few days later that some minor crime was committed in Arangaon, and the ancient feud flared up; one village party was on the point of killing the other when they remembered Baba. They sent a delegation to Him, saying that only Meher Baba could settle their differences. He returned word that He would meet a contingent from either side, both at the same time, at the ashram in Meherabad that evening.

As we rode up, the two parties were seated, divided on either side of the building, and Baba arranged that they were kept waiting for a few moments and then suddenly called into the ashram. In this way they came inside all mixed as one party and Baba requested them at once to be seated on the floor.

One villager with murderous thoughts against the other found himself seated next to one of the opposite party—but they were so intent upon putting their side of the question before Meher Baba, believing Him to be the True Judge, that they did what on other occasions would have been impossible without bloodshed.

Baba had several of His able, staunch men disciples conduct the gathering, and if more than one villager spoke at a time they were quietly but strongly kept in order. Baba showed extreme patience and listened to about forty anguished souls with all they had to say. Finally one old woman came forward and swayed back and forth, almost as if she were reciting an incantation of all the woes of the race. One of the village men stepped forward and pushed her aside, as even they could not stand so many woes!

At another point, when evidently the particular offender was speaking, about ten men arose and commenced yelling at one another. Baba smiled benignly and then clapped His hands for silence. The effect was instantaneous and amazing; the men so rough and loud and Baba so gentle in comparison, not speaking, but with only a hand clap of command that abated their storm of passion.

On His board, interpreted by one of His disciples, He informed the gathering that, as evidently they had made up their minds not to be peaceable, there was nothing to do but to leave the matter to take its course, and when it reached the authorities they would deal with it in their own way. Baba arose to leave. Upon this the villagers, who were enjoying their ill feelings towards one another and wished to talk all night, were taken aback and their faces visibly fell, for suddenly the arguers were left without an argument, as fire without fuel!

Meher Baba paused at the doorway and, seeing them crestfallen, stated that He would remain only if they would abide by His decision—to which they agreed. First He took the headman to task for not having kept better order in the village. Some began to feel rather sorry because they felt in their hearts that they were really to blame in the matter. Then He told the dissenters that they must **"forgive and forget and become one."**

As long as they had two parties they could never accomplish this. There was much discussion amongst themselves, and I thought, of course, that they were objecting to giving up the two parties; but instead there was objection to eating together, as it had been proposed that a village feast be held. The question at issue appeared to be that one side would not accept food from the other. In Indian custom if both parties agree to eat together, it becomes a bond; similarly, in our Christian Bible it refers to breaking bread together as something sacred; but we in the West have lost the significance that the East still has for this rite.

It was agreed finally that if Meher Baba Himself would give the food, they would both accept from Him and thereby become one family. In this concrete manner, a few days later, Baba thus blessed this flock of black and white sheep, uniting them from ancient hatred into fellowship.

On the twenty-sixth of November last, as the Arangaon villagers wished to express their appreciation to Baba and to cement their union by coming to Him, a gathering was arranged which commenced at sunset time. A long line consisting of the four hundred inhabitants, together with their children, came up the hill where we were residing, led by their musicians who kept time in a slow rhythm of dance. Baba was seated on the ground in front of the place where once He had retired in seclusion for a year, and where there now is erected, over His cave, a white domed structure.

The evening ceremony consisted of a bhajan, or sacred recital, sung before Baba. Until now the former parties had kept back one thing, which Meher Baba knew, and that was sitting next to each other in the temple. Instead they held the weekly bhajans separately. This sacred song recital in Baba's presence commenced by one of the former parties singing, accompanied by bell-like instruments; and then that which had not happened for years occurred: the other party joined in unison.

At this point Baba, who knows so well the childlike need of the people for a material symbol, gave to the villagers a long-shaped drum, which is an ancient sign of the "peace of unity." Hereafter at the bhajan in the temple they will sing together accompanied by its rhythmic beat, which in their orchestration is played as recurrently as the beat of the human heart.

All the assembly of men, women and children came forward to receive Meher Baba's darshan and prasad before returning to their homes; and they took leave with song and blessings in their hearts.

MEHER BABA JOURNAL
May 1939

Spiritual Journey with a Modern Guru(Blue Bus Tour)
Part I

by Elizabeth Patterson

The East preserves its ancient traditions as living realities and its spiritual memories as facts that can happen again today. One of the traditional actualities reverenced since remote eras is that of the spiritual relationship of guru (Master) and chela (disciple). While we of the West have generally little cognizance of the matter, the precedent for this tradition has been brought to us through the five great religions of universal acceptance, all of which interestingly enough have the Orient as their background. These scriptures respectively give evidence of the closeness of the bond between Master and disciple, as well as telling of their journeyings together. The great gurus taught and trained their circle of close disciples not so much by teaching as through their own radiant example of perfected living on this earth while journeying along life's highway and byway. The spiritual path to God has ever a counter reflection in the spiritual world.

To try to relate something of an unusual journey, taken in these recent times with a modern Sadguru through the spiritual centers of India, can be at best but a limited telling, as His unlimited realms of spiritual working are beyond human comprehension. Even on the material plane no one disciple can possibly take part in all the Master's manifold activities. His journeyings sow the seeds of spirituality. Time conceals much of what a Master *does*, but reveals in true light what a Master *is*; for His very being makes every act, however seemingly commonplace at the moment, an abiding reality beyond time and place.

Particularly for Westerners, to visualize something of this spiritual tour it must be pictured against the background of the eternal East, though it is but a focal point for the regenerating seeds of spirituality to be planted for coming times. Meher Baba's approach to any people or any subject, whether Eastern or Western, is modern. *Truth is ever new.*

India, the scene of this present spiritual journey, is the great Aryan Mother, and her children are manifold. In fact, I believe her to be the primordial ancestor that rocked the cradle when the five races of mankind were in their infancy. No doubt because of this close relationship of races in India, not anyone native to her soil today considers any difference in races as such; for they are *all* Indian, though dating back from the time of various invasions of this vast land, which has a way of eventually absorbing its conquerors—as a mother wins back her children. Every country has its divisions in some form or other, and India is divided through its religions and sub-divisions of religions. Each conqueror brought with him his own religion, and it became transplanted into the Indian soil; and along with it was brought its kindred traditions and culture. Therefore one finds today a tremendous wealth of religions and cultures that, despite the passing of ages, are not dead, or found only through excavation, but still are a vital part of the everyday life of the people. One feels the infinite possibility in India that *what was, still is.* The unbroken link with humanity's past is still being forged.

Before Christ walked this earth, spirituality had flowered several times in India through Avataric manifestations that left their inspiration and imprint clearly traceable to this day. Thousands of years of fervent religious striving could not fail among the people to bear fruit; and today there exist some of the greatest spiritual saints, as well as religious rogues.

"There is in India the highest and the lowest," Meher Baba has told His disciples.

Part of the reason for this present spiritual journey, the modern Master has stated, is for Him to encounter saints and evolved souls whom He already knows, but wants personally to contact at this particular time. He has further stated that **"the importance of saints is that they point so many to God."** All spiritually minded people cannot but agree that the world never needed the beneficial influence of saints more than now. All true saints function together as one, in divinity.

Another part of the reason for this journey is for the Master to train His disciples and prepare them for His greater work to come. Giving a description in some detail of various events which occurred on the tour of the spiritual centers of India, it might be useful to quote here from my diary:

Early in the morning of the 8th of December 1938, we leave the ashram at Meherabad with Meher Baba—twenty-two of us—in a motorbus specially designed for this extensive tour throughout India. None of the disciples know the Master's plans, other than that Hyderabad (Nizam's Dominions) will be our first place of stay; and that we may be gone for as long as six months, traveling from Central India to points which might eventually include the Himalayas—all according to His spiritual design. Details and schedules are unimportant when we travel with a Master who is the center of the universe of our spirit. Whether one goes or whether one stays, life's wheel, to us, has the same great hub. We are aware that our journey in reality is inward in Truth, although Baba gives it a symbol of outward expression.

The blue bus is heavily laden with luggage and some cooking equipment, which the Eastern and Western disciples at the outset consider necessary for travel through the cool of winter and the heat of summer, which in India follow one another in swift succession. Anticipation holds sway as all crowd into the bus and depart exactly at the moment designated beforehand by Baba. Those at the ashram for whom other plans of work are to be carried out wave goodbye to the Master with deep feeling, although knowing that His internal guidance is ever with them, no matter the distance separating.

The blue bus, loaded and ready for departure, 1937.

The first stop for the night is at Sholapur, in a Rest House near the railroad station. Owing to the heavy luggage load, which is later lightened, motoring is slow and we arrive late. As we are to start early next morning it is thought best by Baba that the bedding-rolls on top of the bus should not be unpacked, so we sleep as well as we can, on a few tables, large chairs or on the floor, with only our overcoats to cover us in the coolness of a December night—an indication that the trip is not going to be only a "bed of roses." Baba, however, in His inimitable way, looks to everyone's feeling, moods and health, as the great Engineer of Life ever keeps the mechanics of living in order.

Next day we continue into Hyderabad State, and after passing the border we picnic along the shore of a river. Baba, who enlivens every situation, makes us feel gay and responsive to nature around us, although the country is merely rocky land and many are feeling cramped in the crowded bus. Some differences in scenery from the great plateau draw our attention along the way, and every now and then we see groves of toddy palms with vessels hanging to their cut barks to catch the sweet juices. Occasionally there are very large irrigated rice fields, with water buffalos drawing the cultivators in their slow, majestic pace. Approaching Hyderabad, the Mohammedan city dating back to the great Mogul times, it is in the rocks themselves, especially the enormous rounded ones pinnacled on the adjacent hill-tops, that one can perceive the antiquity of the surroundings. Long before the Mogul period these stone giants stood sentinel.

Those in the Master's party were to be the guests of the ex-Prime Minister of Hyderabad, but owing to triple circumstances, one of which was the occurrence of plague for the first time in the history of the village adjoining his estate, arrangements are hastily made to stay on another of his estates that has been closed for some time. The dwelling being an antique palace originally used for Mohammedan women observing the purdah custom, it is thought that this place will give Baba and His party the privacy He has requested for the sojourn.

It turns out that we are to spend only one night in this ancient palace, which is devoid of all furnishings (though an offer to bring furniture the next day is made). This night, however, is made memorable by the eerie feeling one often senses in a dwelling of antiquity, and the lines of the poet came to my mind: "Those who dwell in marble halls and ancient palace old in story." The unusually gay and mirthful spirit of Baba causes all to respond, and soon the place is ringing with life and laughter. Presently the gracious wife of the official deputed for our reception brings to us caldrons of hot food from her own home, and after meeting the Master spontaneously volunteers to continue to supervise cooking arrangements for the entire stay of the party.

. . . Events with the Master move quickly. The next morning He is off in a motor car with the official, and by 10 a.m. they have returned. Baba announces to us that we are all to move that very afternoon, as the residence of the Nizam's brother, which at present is unoccupied and is located not far from the heart of the city, and with the seclusion of a large garden, has been put at the Master's disposal for the sojourn. There is plenty of room for our large party, some others of which have subsequently arrived by train. Among these is Mohammed, who has been brought over from the Ashram for the "God-mad" at Meherabad, and who is a special type of spiritually dazed soul whom the Master considers an important link with future work along this line which will be continued throughout the trip.

The stay in Hyderabad might be termed a time of *stirring* by the Master, more than outward working. During this period one also feels, as well as sees, the indications that the Master is preoccupied with *internal* spiritual work.

. . . A fact that indicates clearly that this ancient State is rich in spiritual history is that there is a street in Hyderabad City called the "Street of the Saints." Here the past spiritual lineage is buried, and it is a constant place of pilgrimage by those of various religions. The present Nizam is spiritually minded, and many of his predecessors were notedly so, and have always had spiritual advisors to the throne. Outside of the city are two places of interest, located on high opposite hills, one of which is the great and picturesque palace reserved for the King Emperor when he should visit Hyderabad State. The other is the rocky abode for visiting saints, pinnacled high against the blue sky.

When making the tour with His disciples one day to these parts, the Master has the bus turn around near the base of the steep steps leading up to the abode for saints. Here, seated humbly at the base, is a man, looking much like a pilgrim lost in contemplation of divinity, who Baba said was truly a spiritual soul, well advanced on the Path. The Master gives this man a glance which seems to cause a light of rare happiness to pass across the countenance of the seated figure, who visibly shows an expression of inner recognition.

The Master had, previous to our arrival in Hyderabad, told His disciples that there is a true saint living in the ancient city. Out of interest some of these disciples now question a few local people who seem well versed in the spiritual history of the place; but they are very reticent about the matter, although one admits that there is a woman saint who is impossible to find.

Shortly before our departure, the Master, who knows all saints, sends out one of His disciples, who for years led an ascetic life under Baba's spiritual direction, to search out the saint. Baba often uses disciples to establish contact, and they are sent out without any specific information as to the whereabouts, but inevitably they seem to walk right to the place. This woman saint, it seems, lives in the poorest and most crowded part of the city, in an obscure back courtyard. She is in a state of super-consciousness, rarely functioning on the gross plane. Although constantly surrounded by crowds of devotees seated quietly around her, she does not give advice or guidance—but India knows well the beneficial influence of spiritual *being*, and does not lay the stress on mere *doing*, which Westerners are apt to consider of prime importance. Baba Himself does not find need to visit this saint, but sends with the aforementioned disciple two of His Western disciples on a second day. Those around the saint are averse to foreigners approaching her, but in her peculiar way she beckons the three disciples of Baba's to be seated near her, and strangely enough permits the Westerners to photograph her, which they do with deference. Later, upon seeing the photograph, I was struck by the expression of her eyes, like a female John the Baptist. She was as rigid as a statue, her hair was matted, and she wore only a loin-cloth. Her face, inclined towards heaven, blazed with the fire of spiritual intensity.

Shortly afterwards, the Master, declaring that He has finished the spiritual work that He came to do in Hyderabad, gives the signal that we are all leaving the following day after only ten days sojourn.

The surprise to the disciples and to the outsiders who had become interested in the Master's plans for a spiritual center here is due to the fact that the plans seemed maturing, and materially speaking it seems an inopportune time to leave. Yet Masters, as we surely know, have a universal vision which comprises the *whole* scheme of things and not only the *part*. Events in time bring this out, even to the eyes of ordinary mortals.

Spiritual Journey with a Modern Guru (Blue Bus Tour)
Part II
by Elizabeth Patterson

How often it is told in the New Testament that Christ stayed in a home of one of His disciples! The life of a Master is, in the very nature of His high calling, one of transience while on this earth. The love in the heart of a disciple and the spiritual need of humanity are two of the strongest drawing powers that bring a Master towards a longing soul.

Meher Baba's next place of stay on our uncharted journey was in a home of one of His disciples at Jubbulpore (Central Provinces). The arrangements were impromptu, as all had thought that the Master would remain for a considerable period in Hyderabad, and none knew the route of the six-month motor tour except that Baba with His disciples would visit the spiritual centers of India. Yet with the shortest notice everything was made ready at Jubbulpore by a disciple there for an indefinite stay for our large group; for "with love all things are possible."

On our way north a brief stopover was made at Nagpur, also in the home of a disciple. Those who chanced to hear of the Master's presence in Nagpur came for His darshan, to lay their heads on His sacred feet. This hallowed custom in the East dates from time immemorial, just as the age-old blessing of the laying-on of hands was known in the Near East long before the advent of Christ. The act of blessing which was adopted by the western Church signifies two meanings in one: "the bestowal of divine favor" and "to make happy"; while darshan implies the absolving of one's sanskaras (or impressions) which veil the mind and keep the soul from seeing God. If the presence of a Sadguru or Perfect Master is known in India His grace is eagerly sought; and during the short stay at Nagpur a crowd gathered outside the gate of the compound for the chance of receiving Meher Baba's darshan. In this regard Baba once said: **"Many come but very rare are the real lovers of God."** Yet this implies that they *do* exist.

An incident did not escape my notice that, while Baba was receiving some devotees who had known Him for years, a constantly repeated sacred chant which always ended in *Meher Baba Ki Jai!* was being sung by some ascetic outside the gate. Even during the night before, the distant sound of this refrain had come to our ears through the stillness of the night air. As our party left for Jubbulpore, Baba gave all the assembled crowd an opportunity to take His darshan, and when a tall ascetic with very bright eyes came forward I recognized him as the same one whom I had seen on the day of Baba's Birthday at Ahmednagar. On that occasion last February one of the disciples from Nagpur told me that she had just spoken to this man, and that, two months before, he had come to the door of her family home at Nagpur where Baba had been staying, but he had arrived after the Master's departure. When told that Baba had left for Ahmednagar the tall ascetic stood transfixed.

Hours afterwards she glanced out of her window and saw the man standing in the same spot with tears in his eyes, looking as if he had searched years and missed the chance of a lifetime. Then two months later she saw him again in distant Meherabad and, upon questioning the ascetic, she learned that he had left Nagpur on foot the very day of being told of the Master's departure, arriving in Ahmednagar, as good fortune would have it, on the very day of Baba's Birthday. The ascetic's face clearly showed the bliss of the encounter with the Master. For those who truly seek with steadfastness, patience and a song in the heart, how small a moment it takes in the presence of a Master to realize the *divine reality* which has been the search of years!

. . . Through the active occupations and experiences of everyday life, the constant training of Baba's disciples goes on at Jubbulpore as elsewhere. Rarely does the Master give what might be termed a discourse or lecture. All this the institutions and learned books of the world can give in abundance, but it is in the example of life itself that Baba makes one aware of the higher values and meanings behind even the petty happenings that daily tend to obscure the vision of God. It is easy to be infused through sermons and inspirational talks once or twice a week and return home elevated in mind and spirit. Then something happens, perhaps a very small incident of mundane life which causes annoyance, and one becomes irritated or angry. One's inspired mood is spoiled, and one sinks again to the level of week-day living, waiting for the Sabbath day to restore again holier thoughts and to elevate one's spirit. Under Baba's guidance, however, there is no let-up in the training of spirituality as applied to everyday life itself.

Christ's own way of teaching His disciples was by making the smallest happening a vital awakening to life's spiritual meanings. He drew His examples from the ordinary things which occurred along the daily path He trod, such as "a grain of mustard seed," "a house built upon the sand" or "the lost sheep." Such awakening to spiritual values behind the common things of life is ever the way of the teaching of Masters. Their own example of perfected living on

Meher Baba at Jubbulpore, 1938.

this earth was more potent than scriptures, the writing of which they left to others. Meher Baba once told His disciples, making objective use of a dispute which had occurred between two persons:

"All the meditations, yogas, concentrations do not teach what Baba teaches you through everyday living; that is, to be kind to those who ill-treat you and to love those whom you dislike. This is the highest practice of yoga. When Christ was mocked, spat upon and beaten, He did not use His powers but He retaliated with love. You should be glad of an opportunity to be mistreated by others; you should thank them for the opportunity of suffering and loving. The purpose of your being with Baba is to eliminate the ego."

The loaded blue bus crosses the Indus River en route to Quetta.

An interesting event took place at the beginning of the year 1939. Upasni Maharaj, Meher Baba's second Master, who was touring with his disciples at practically the same time in the same general direction as Baba, crossed through Jubbulpore on his return to Sakori. No meeting between these two Masters was necessary, for they are one in the realms of higher consciousness; but Maharaj sent one of his disciples to Baba's disciples with the message: "Tell Merwan that this day I passed through His house." The exact meaning of this mystical phrase is known only to Baba Himself. The event, however, of the paths of the two Masters crossing makes one ponder the fact that these two currents of spirituality should fuse at such a materialistic time in the world. Perhaps the period for spiritual re-ascendancy may be near!

The next stop on our journey is Benares, one of the most ancient of spiritual centers in this age-old land. To be with the Master under such circumstances is indeed to wonder at one's own privilege! India I have seen before—any traveler can see India—but few can *feel* it; still fewer can perceive its spiritual currents or understand anything of their trend. For I believe that India is the spiritual "barometer" for the world's religious currents.

It was twelve years ago that I originally went to Benares, that holy city where the Ganges flows, and with other passengers from an around-the-world cruise saw the principal places of interest. At Benares thousands upon thousands of pilgrims from every corner of India came to bathe in the sacred waters. It was a cross section of life in its aspect of devotion—rogues wished to be absolved of their sins and seekers wished to find God. Of all this picturesque multitude, one memory remains most vividly in my mind. It was the look in the eyes of an old woman of

Meher Baba (wearing Elizabeth's coat) at Benares, 1939.

over eighty years when she first saw the holy Ganges. Poverty and paralysis could not daunt her spirit; her grandson, a young man, had carried her on his back for four hundred miles—to fulfill her life's desire. That look of rapture, oblivious of all else save the sacred waters, was unforgettable. But was it the river itself, or perhaps had God entered her soul at that moment; who knows? Whatever it was that caused the sight of the Ganges to bring such extraordinary rapture to her ancient eyes, at the same time brought to my traveler's sense the knowledge that what I saw was only external. How much I was missing! I thought that if ever I did come to India again, it must be to see what to me was now unseen, yet to the earnest pilgrims was so tangible and real.

My second visit to Benares just now with the Master is the fulfillment of that wish, and it has made me perceive that it is not the waters but the spiritual atmosphere of the locality. Those in the West who have stayed at Assisi, Italy, will understand something of what I mean by spiritual atmosphere; for the life of St. Francis has left vibrations and a rarefied purity that one actually experiences. Meher Baba told His disciples:

"What there is about Benares, or Kashi as it was earlier called, is the atmosphere of great souls. Rama, Krishna, Buddha, Christ, Shankara—all were here for a period of their lives."

The spiritual history of Benares dates back at least three thousand years, probably longer; and the indelible imprints of these founders of religions can be the greater apprehended as one proceeds along the spiritual path. Also Kabir, the great mystic and poet, drew his inspiration from these parts.

When we were riding with Meher Baba in a boat on the Ganges, He seemed preoccupied with spiritual working. Later He remarked: **"There never was a time when this ancient place did not have true saints. Even though the priests of all castes may be there like vultures to take materially from the pilgrims, they cannot despoil the spiritual atmosphere."**

One of His disciples inquired, "How about the believers who come in search of God and are like sheep shorn by those who are false priests? Is it better to have faith and be disillusioned or have no faith?"

Meher Baba replied **"Any faith with the idea of truth behind it is better than no faith at all. It is better to walk the wrong road and return to the right way than not to walk at all. What matters spiritually is faith. When faith becomes love then there is no need for faith any longer."**

At either end of the *ghats* or steep steps leading down to the water's edge, which extend for several miles, there lives today an advanced soul who for years has remained there. These "soldiers of God," as Baba calls them, are the silent sentries. The torch of spirituality is kept burning through their pure existence. They live in places almost inaccessible, and few can know them. The time has come, the Master remarked, for Him to marshal these and other "soldiers of God," so that is why He personally came to contact them. Someone asked Baba: "Why, since You are a Master and they are so advanced, or are saints, need You trouble to contact them in person?" The Master explained: **"They already know Me, but it is for My work that it is needed."**

Buddha was the ruler in His epoch and He resigned His throne to seek God. After many years of wandering in the jungles and mountains He reached the spiritual Goal and received Enlightenment (God-realization). It was near

Benares where He gathered His first disciples and commenced His teachings. Today there are remaining at Sarnath, eight miles back from the Ganges, interesting architectural and sculptural remains of the spiritual center which grew up around His abode. A gigantic stupa which looms up against the sky contains, as do all Buddhistic stupas, a relic of the Master. This great dome-like edifice evidently was built by the disciples after Buddha's passing away. The beautiful statues of Buddha now preserved by the government all belong to a later period, for it is generally believed that the use of idols in worship came into the religion at a much later date.

This experience of visiting the holy place in the company of the Master of this epoch made the scene very living and real. Meher Baba remarked in passing: **"I remember every detail."**

Spiritual Journey with a Modern Guru (Blue Bus Tour)
Part III
by Elizabeth Patterson

"Delhi dur hai" has been a saying in India for the last five hundred years. Its literal meaning is "Delhi is far"; but the phrase came to have an import of fate behind it after being originally uttered by one whom time has called a saint. This holy man lived in Delhi centuries ago and had fallen into disfavor with the king—perhaps for his capacity of speaking the truth and for his predictions which made him feared by this ruler. In any case, once when the king was away on conquests, which brought him a series of successes even as far away as Bengal, he did not like to hear the reports of the saint's growing influence at home; so he sent word that he should leave Delhi before the royal return. In reply to the victorious king, who was even then on the march back to his capital, the saint sent the above cryptic reply.

The proud king, just before his arrival at the gates of Delhi, desired to celebrate his renowned victories and staged a great pageantry on the plains surrounding the capital, which had been the scene of many an ancient victory and defeat. Among the other things arranged was an elephant fight between the king's own battling herds; and during the terrific struggle that ensued, which delighted the ruler very much, one of the battling elephants became enraged and, dashing out of all control, charged the very place where the king was reviewing the fight, and instantly killed the monarch. Thus the words of the saint, "Delhi dur hai," took on dramatic significance.

This picturesque anecdote is told because it tends somewhat to illustrate the constant play of good and evil forces that have been the background of Delhi, which was our next place of stay on the spiritual journey through India with a modern Sadguru.

From the 12th century up to the advent of the present new Imperial capital, there have been seven dynasties. The past history of Delhi includes rulers with their conquests, but interwoven with the carnage of battles is the gentle tradition of saints. Why, we may ask, should these evolved souls be found amongst such material surroundings? Or could we not elicit more enlightenment if rather we asked, why should we not find saints where there is great spiritual need? That a lineage of saints did have their abodes around this ancient country we can find precedents for in our Biblical scriptures, where it is stated that there was a long line of prophets around Jerusalem for centuries; and Palestine was no more spiritual a land in those days than India.

Outside of Delhi today, about fifteen miles distant, there stands one of the most perfect of architectural columns, with five stories towering gracefully towards the heavens. It is called Kutub Minar. Going to this monument one day in early February 1939 with Meher Baba, the party of disciples passed near the old city of Delhi, which was build on the site of the most remote capital, that dated back to the 1st century. This date, in comparison, would have been the time of the early Christians following the Resurrection. Feeling the atmosphere of the past as we gazed at the almost ethereal beauty of the Kutub Minar, Meher Baba linked the column with the present existence by remarking that the Kutub Minar has importance today not only in the material world but in the subtle world.

A few miles away on our return ride to Delhi in the bus, which had been our faithful conveyance throughout the journey, Baba directed that we stop at the shrine of Nizam-ud-Din, a 14th-century saint who is much revered even today by countless pilgrims. First we were shown the saint's last earthly resting place, which had been also the site of his abode. An incident related by the guardian of the shrine gave reality to the past in the imagination of Baba's disciples. He pointed out a nearby grave which was simply covered over by grass and told us that nothing but fresh grass is ever put on the small plot, as this was the express wish of Jehanara, the daughter of Shah Jehan, the great Mogul Emperor and builder of the Taj Mahal. She left court life to become a disciple of the saint, Nizam-ud-Din, and it was her desire, having renounced everything in the world for the life of the spirit, that no kind of commemoration be placed on her grave, not even flowers. While the earthly distinctions to which she was born meant nothing to her, it might well have pleased her to have her last resting place in close proximity to the shrine of the great saint who had been her spiritual Master.

Before coming to Delhi, Meher Baba had remarked to his disciples that they might see there a living saint who was one of his spiritual agents. As the shrine of Nizam-ud-Din was known to be the tomb of a past saint, this was the place where we least expected the privilege of seeing a living saint. But in journeying with the Master surprises were the order of the day. We were led by Baba to an out-of-the-way, cell-like chamber within the large enclosure where dwells, in the shadow of the shrine, a patriarchal holy man with grey beard and extraordinarily luminous eyes.

Only a shaft of light entered through the doorway where we stood with the Master, but fortunately for us, it fell directly upon the noble features of one who resembled our ideal of the prophets of old. We witnessed the expression of deep inner recognition as this saint beheld the Master. We knew that the normal human eye with its limited sight has the capacity of seeing only the material body; but what of the inner sight of the subtle eye and the vision of the spiritual, both of which are said to be possessed by saints? What light effulgent must they behold in a Master!

The Master himself has stated that only a Master can truly recognize a Master, but indeed what this saint perceived at that moment in Baba was a spiritual experience which we felt with reverence. In our less developed way, we could join in concord with the saint; as we so deeply knew in our hearts concerning Meher Baba that, in the words of the simple faith of Mary Magdalene about Christ: "He is one not as other men are."

Meher Baba, upon leaving the holy dweller of the shrine, told us that the saint is the spiritual guardian of this district, and at that very moment he had received a spiritual promotion through contact with a Master. We might well attach added significance to the fact that it should happen at this period of outer world stress and strain, before the coming spiritual awakening which is now being stirred by the Master.

It was at Delhi that a special trend of Baba's spiritual work during the tour became visible. This was His personal contact and work with masts. Masts are those seekers of God who become dazed upon the Path, whereby their minds become

Elizabeth Patterson with Kippy and a pet lamb at Alwar, India, February 1938.

unbalanced. They are spiritually advanced souls and in India they are known as the "God-intoxicated." I have not heard this latter term used in the West, except concerning some of the early Quakers who became so ecstatic in their devotion and worship of God that they were said to be "intoxicated by the spirit." (This was generally of short duration and not a permanent condition.) Except for a few of the mystics in the West, I do not think that this type is to be found there because the countries are too young, and it is not yet that men go mad there for love of God.

The only hope of cure for the masts is "spiritual cure," and this can only be done by a Perfect Master who has himself arrived at the Goal and can point the way to others. Lesser guides may themselves lose the way to Perfection. A Perfect Master can judge whether it is individually best for a spiritually dazed soul to be gradually brought back to a state of normality on the physical plane or given a spiritual push on the inner planes; and it is He alone who can perform this spiritual service. If such a soul, longing for God, seeking so profoundly, had come originally in contact with a Sadguru, who is a Perfect Guide, he would have been led safely through the "pitfalls" of the spiritual Path, about which every saint has warned the true seekers of God. (Our western names for some of the spiritual pitfalls are pride, greed and lust; therefore, are we not all in need of a Perfect Guide?)

One day, while the disciples were on a drive with Meher Baba through the main parts of the capital, we came to an especially crowded section near the great Mosque which is in about the center of the city. Baba motioned that the bus should be driven close to the wide steps that lead up to this sanctuary. There, amongst the poor, the lame, the halt and the blind who habituate this place in hope of material or spiritual benefit, the Master singled out one soul whom we saw quite a distance away, seated, in ragged garments. Immediately afterwards Baba declared that the drive was at an end, so we all returned to the place where we were residing in Delhi. There Baba directed two of his mandali who had not been on the drive to go and bring this mast from the Mosque.

When they arrived at the steps of the Mosque, they found it most difficult from the description to pick out the right man, as all seemed to answer to the outer description of ragged garment, dark hair, beard, etc. But they were not on the first mission of this kind, for Baba has had some of his mandali searching out masts for the past two years, having them brought to him at the "Ashram for God-mad" at Rahuri and later at Meherabad; so they knew that the Master would enable them to have the right intuition in the matter. Watching all these derelicts of humanity intently, they finally narrowed down the selection to two men. One man seemed to have a spiritual-looking face, and they believed him to be the one until they asked him a question, to which he replied with a tale of having lost his money and position—which sounded all too rational! So turning to the other man, whose only distinguishing feature was that he was inconspicuous, they asked him questions, and his only response to everything was the name of God.

The mandali brought this dazed soul to Meher Baba. When he approached the Master he became like one intoxicated, and his legs failed him, so that he had to be supported. The Master gave him a bath, which carried with it a benediction, as He usually employs the medium of water for the outward "cure" while His personal touch is the medium for spiritual cure. Afterward the man recognized the Master, declaring that that day he had seen the vision of the God whom he had been ceaselessly naming. Baba sent him out again into life, but those who have had long experience with the Master know the spiritual process. Many of these souls automatically, as if through coincidence, are brought again into His contact at a future time and the change is clearly written on their whole being. The Master has bestowed upon them the divine impulse, and life itself has been the school. They become useful mediums for the spreading of the spirit, in the realm of which even his close disciples cannot function.

After leaving Delhi, the Master's party went to Ajmer (Rajputana) via Alwar and Jaipur states. The country we motored through was interesting and one became again aware of the variety and spaciousness of the land which is India. To a large extent the independent states have retained their own character and distinctiveness; one might call them the most picturesque, for they have less of the British influence and are not as much advanced from the modern point of view.

Jaipur is called the "Pink City," as the rocks on which it is situated and the buildings are all of varying shades of pink. Ambar is the ancient city one passes a few miles before coming to the present capital called Jaipur City. Baba remarked that Ambar was the abode of a few evolved souls in the past, and even today there is one who has his abode there.

Rising high above the ancient capital is a great feudal castle that is one of the largest and most picturesque in India. It resembles a fairy-tale version of a city. Just as we were motoring by, we saw a crowd and heard martial music. Then we noticed marching up the steep hill to the upper city the type of troops one associates with "toy soldiers"; they were wearing red trousers, blue coats and large black helmets, and were "goose stepping" very stiffly. When our bus was stopped by traffic we asked what the celebration was, and the police officer replied that the Maharajah was going to worship, and he was being escorted by soldiers.

This police officer seemed unusually interested that our party should view the spectacle, and he pointed to a place where there was a deserted terrace. Baba ordered that we all get out of the bus, apparently to see the sight. One pedestrian passed Baba on the road at that moment, whom we did not remember until afterward, as the disciples' attention was principally focussed on the "taxi stand" down below where there were standing elephants in regal attire for riding, alongside the motor conveyances.

As we watched all the "passing show" of Maya, we felt Baba abstracted. After a few moments He remarked on His board, **"I wanted to stop here,"** and looking at the Master we followed His gaze up to the hill on the opposite side of the procession.

There, outlined against the sky in the clear atmosphere of the mountains, was a sunburnt, weather-beaten man with white hair and beard, wearing only a loin cloth, and with a staff in his hand, who was ascending the path. This ragged man had the far gaze that one finds characteristic of "children of nature" and of mystics. All of a sudden we realized that this man was the same pedestrian who had passed at the very moment that Baba had descended from the bus, and the coincidence naturally struck us, although at the time we had been too engrossed elsewhere to give any attention to this passer-by. Baba, however, who is aware of every passing soul, foreknew this meeting, I felt certain, for I recalled His telling us before we came to Ambar to stop a moment on the other side of the old capital. Until that particular point there had been no opportunity for stopping, due to the unusual circumstances of crowds and police line.

Later Baba informed us that this was the one truly spiritual man of this district, that he is a real lover of God, and does here the Master's spiritual work.

Spiritual Journey with a Modern Guru (Blue Bus Tour)
Part IV
by Elizabeth Patterson

One of the exceptional parts of our tour was that a few hours after arrival at any of the places selected by Meher Baba for our stay, we were ensconced in the new abode almost as if we had not left the former place. With a party of about thirty persons, both Eastern and Western, our number augmented at times by certain other persons assigned on various duties joining the Master for a few days, all being shifted, including luggage and necessities for cooking, it was indeed something of a feat to have it work so smoothly. Naturally the good management and ease in adjustment to new conditions was due to the Master's inspiration, which touched always the smallest details of our lives, and which acted like oil in the otherwise complicated machinery of our migratory existence.

Since leaving the Central Provinces early in 1939, our abodes had been bungalows that were obtained for the period of our stay and selected for their seclusion, although often in the central parts of the cities, as it seemed that Meher Baba did not want to be removed from the swarm of humanity. Outside our gates we were constantly aware of the sounds of passing feet, bullock carts, donkeys, camels and the swift rush of motor cars and lorries laden with passengers; and through all this one sensed that the Master was aware of the heartbeat of each of these striving, straining, hurried souls who were unconscious of His presence, but were nonetheless in His spiritual environment. The dumb creatures, too, did not escape the benediction of His holy presence.

It might be said that the journey itself was but a pause in the rhythm of our ashram life; or, as "life's a stage and we are but the players thereof," according to Shakespearean wisdom, similarly our spiritual training was continuous and only the setting changed. The Master Director assigned the roles, and each played their own according to their capacities.

Certainly part of Meher Baba's training is to develop our "peace within," though in the midst of active, pulsating life. Seclusion, when given by the Master to one of His disciples, is for the better fulfillment of the work at hand and not for personal satisfaction. However, solitude was not our part during this six-month journey. This is what outsiders sometimes have difficulty understanding, as they seem to expect spiritual living to be a cloistered existence with inward contemplation. But Meher Baba leads us along the path in service of others. Some give the service of art or writing; some directly participate in the Master's external work among humanity; others give menial services. As St. Teresa has expressed it: "If obedience employs you in outward things, know that even if you are in the kitchen, our Lord moves amidst the pots and pans, helping us both within and without." Whatsoever the duty, the first step in the field of service is to think of others more than oneself; and the last step is to truly love all others more than oneself. Christ, who had completely transcended the ego, gave love to those who crucified Him. This is the state of perfection.

It would seem that Meher Baba's spiritual work of the tour had reached its highest pitch during the

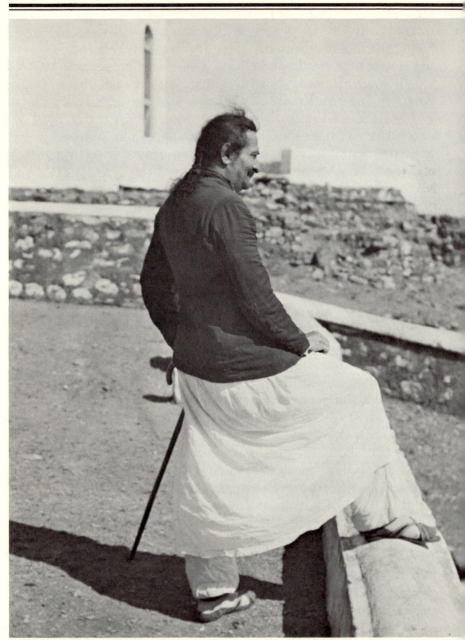

Meher Baba at Turagarh Hill, Ajmer, India, February 1939.

stay at Ajmer (Rajputana). There were so many sidelights to the great searchlight turned on there by the Master that it was utterly impossible for an ordinary individual to follow all; but each disciple sensed it in his own way and felt its import and momentum as at no other place on this journey of spiritual experience. At Ajmer the Master particularly was on a search for souls—lost souls, advanced souls, mad souls, spiritually-dazed souls, and those who had attained the stage of sainthood. When Meher Baba *stirs*, events and circumstances move quickly.

From the earthly point of view one could call the Master's activities a search; from the spiritual pattern each of these destined souls were but "coming into their own." The appointed hour for them to meet the Master had come—no clockwork could be more precise, no fate more accurate. The rare souls on a plane of spiritual advancement, with whom intuition had become Knowledge, knew beforehand of the Master's coming, and only the outer contact had yet to be made. Others less advanced on the Path were intuitively drawn towards Meher Baba by circumstances that might ordinarily be termed coincidence. Still others, unconscious as to the cause behind their inward spiritual longing, came, as would the blind, led by the helping hand of another. The lost souls seemed just of themselves to stray like sheep into the fold; while the erratic impulses of the mad, by the law of averages, proved that day to be sane!

A bungalow at Ajmer, arranged in advance for the Master's party, proved to be on a quiet corner, nevertheless just off the main artery leading into the heart of the city. Two of the household were assigned the more strenuous tasks, which for one of them was to prepare food for any number of strange souls who might come to Baba at any hour of the day; and for the other, to prepare hot water over the charcoal burners in large quantities and be ready to carry it herself in bucketfuls, at any moment, for the Master's use in giving the beneficial bath to the selected men.

What strange interweavings of fate Baba brings about! For example, here were two Western women, one from London and the other from New York, serving the spiritually advanced souls of the East in such arduous fashion.

The Master sent His specially chosen men disciples out here and there in Ajmer, at His directions, to fish for souls. The task in its ramifications is unbelievable. One by one, with infinite patience these strange souls are persuaded to leave their nooks and crannies. One of the first located was a man who had sat for four years in the railroad station, where nothing had persuaded him to leave, even when boiling water had been thrown over him by the stationmaster. Finally this official had resigned himself to the fact that there was something unusual in this man, and allotted him a place where he might remain. The man who had taken upon himself the task of doing his spiritual work for humanity in the thoroughfare of a railroad station had still the physical scars of the burns which were meant to dissuade him. Yet he was ultimately brought to Baba after years of being seated in one place.

The Master, working in His own way, did not go out to contact these spiritual men directly. It would have made the task easy for the disciples if these advanced souls could but gaze upon His face. But the disciples must follow Baba's directions implicitly and at the same time be ingenious enough to find the ways and means to carry them out. The disciple in each case had then to tell his own tale and relate the many incidents leading up to the final success of persuading such adamant characters to forsake their accustomed ways, which seem to us so peculiar, and then bringing them over to the bungalow where Baba was staying.

Upon arrival of this spiritual man from the railroad station, the Master bathed and fed him as a little child. (Did Christ not say, "Except ye become as little children, ye cannot enter the Kingdom of Heaven"?) When I first saw the man, he had been clothed by Meher Baba in a new white kafni, and he was seated on a chair in the Master's own room. His short pointed beard, downcast eyes and holy expression reminded me strikingly of the well-known paintings of Christ after the scourging was over and someone had placed a white garment upon Him. The crown of thorns was lacking from the present scene; but the transcendent, meek expression radiated from his face. This innocent, I thought, was daily seated among the judging Sanhedrin and today, possibly for the first time, was without "thorns." Tomorrow again he would be at his railroad station amongst the crowds, but today, in Baba's presence, he looked transfigured.

Why is this beneficial bath by Baba necessary; or for these selected masts, why the feeding with the Master's own hands? To those who believe, it is a spiritual matter understood with the intuition. To those who are privileged to witness such transformation of consciousness as is brought about by the Master through His personal touch, and through the simple mediums of water and food, the matter is one of direct revelation. But to those to whom such matters are alien, I can but refer them to parallels in scriptures of all the great Masters.

In the New Testament of the Christians, water

is used as regenerative force, as in baptism, which is considered to give spiritual re-birth. The simple act of giving of bread by Christ later became a sacrament when at the Last Supper He said: "Take, eat this bread in remembrance of Me." Who can understand with ordinary reasoning the full spiritual import of such happenings on this earth in the days of Christ? We know, however, that the greatness of a Master consists in His taking the common daily things of life, and through His usage they become a blessed sacrament. With every physical symbol is a spiritual meaning. Christ said: "I shall give ye bread from which ye shall never be enhungered and waters from which ye shall never thirst." Since Christ's day these holy acts have become mere rituals of the Church, rather than living realities in everyday life of humanity.

... I witnessed in Ajmer men coming to Meher Baba who had long given up the world for the life of the spirit; who held fast to their own beliefs and faiths, yet were racked and weary, soul-tortured, or dazed upon the Path. I have seen them leave the presence of the Master after the beneficial bath, cleansed in body and in spirit, and with the unmistakable expression of regeneration upon their faces. It was like seeing a garden of humanity, purified and shining, after celestial rains. The stirring of the spirit by the touch of the Master, if one has the privilege to witness it, is far more self evident than when one sees and knows that a man is glad, or a man is sad. This state of bliss cannot be hidden; it radiates from one's very being.

... Before our arrival in Ajmer, Baba had indicated to us that there were two spiritual agents there who were highly evolved souls on the fifth and sixth planes of consciousness, and that they would come to Him during His stay there. Furthermore that we

should see them. Upon hearing this, my mind
recalled the two "sentinels" at either end of the ghats
at Benares who sat in that ancient stronghold of
spirituality continuing the spiritual link with the
ages; and also the saint that we had the rare privilege
of seeing outside of Delhi. Baba had said that these
men were the spiritual guardians of their districts.
When one is with a Master such as Meher Baba,
many scriptural meanings, little understood before,
suddenly become alive and take on actuality in the
present as well as reality in the past. For example,
regarding the spiritual guardianship of a people of a
district, the words of the Prophet Ezekiel took on
new light: "The word of the Lord came upon me,
saying, Son of Man, I have made thee a watchman
unto the house of Israel." The old Testament is
replete with such "watchman" prophets. Now I
thought with conviction, why should only the lands
of the past be so blessed?

This section of Rajputana is one of the most
spiritual in India. In the past a very great saint,
named Khwaja Moenuddin Chisti, worshipped by
Mohammedans and Hindus alike, came from Arabia
and had his abode in this locality. His spiritual
influence was so vast that eventually he died a
martyr to local religious orthodox feeling that was
very fierce in those times. Today Ajmer is
considered, due to his life and martyrdom there, to
be the "Mecca" in India for Mohammedans; and
Hindus also come to worship at his tomb in countless
numbers throughout the year. It proved to be in one
of the narrow streets radiating off the saint's shrine
that one of the spiritual agents referred to by Baba
had his abode.

One day during our three-week stay in Ajmer
the Master took us to visit this ancient sacred place
which at the present time is carefully guarded by

priests who collect all the fees they can. But with it all they cannot spoil the spiritual atmosphere which one senses is very profound. However, the reverence of the Western disciples for the holy life of the past could not be expressed, for the priests would not permit any Westerners to approach the actual resting place. Yet can one complain, for did not the petty prejudices of Western Christians at times call those who worship Eastern religions "heathens"? We today are following One Who in His pure life and spiritual love knows *all* mankind as God's children—as indeed all Perfect Masters of all times have done.

Just as we were leaving the large area of the shrine and had returned to our bus, an ascetic man with glowing eyes passed close to the window where Baba sat. Recognition passed between them, and then we drove off as if nothing special had occurred. Later Baba sent two of His mandali back to this section to search out the man, and he was eventually found, lying in a kind of gutter, completely unconscious of the body and immersed in spiritual bliss. He was brought to the Master and remained throughout the stay.

This man was tall and slim in build, of middle age, and had a noble bearing. During the days with the Master, he appeared always inwardly exalted; his eyes had an intensely burning look, seeming to be seeing things afar. His artistic-looking hands were constantly moving and gesticulating as if in conversation with unseen entities, and sometimes as if he were leading an unheard heavenly choir. His speech, which was rare, seemed disconnected to those of the men disciples who were in attendance; but Baba told us that all that the man uttered had spiritual meaning. Sometimes even at night we would hear him singing in a deep, sonorous voice like the chant of a priest, so loudly that the sound carried through the walls into our quarters. During the days that he stayed under the Master's roof, He bathed him and fed him with His own hands, and at the same time gave him a "spiritual push." This period of sojourn for this child of God was a spiritual home-coming. His state of bliss was extraordinary and continuous.

Meher Baba told us that he was one of His spiritual agents on the fifth plane and that during the time he was with the Master he had been spiritually advanced.

The second spiritual agent in Ajmer was found through the guidance of a tipsy tonga driver. Such strange humans are often pieces in the picture-puzzle which in life seem to fit into no place, but under the influence of a Master such as Meher Baba become the missing and important pieces which complete the picture.

On our journey, whether there were sinners or whether there were saints, they all came to Meher Baba, whose name means Compassionate Father, as little children. That is the most beautiful part of my spiritual experience with a modern Sadguru.

Excerpt from
"Notes from My Diary"
by F. H. Dadachanji

An explanation Meher Baba gave during an interview
to a journalist—Mr. T.A. Raman—was published
in the *Evening News of India* on January 7, 1937, under
the title: "When the World Will Listen."

"Why does not Meher Baba break His self-
imposed silence and preach in the market place? But,
argues the sage, every great change must be
carefully timed. How else could it be with the
greatest revolution in the mind of man? **'The time of
preaching in the market-place will come,'** says
Meher Baba, **'only after the world has been humbled
and purified by a carnage greater than any the world
has yet seen.'**

"This is the prediction which has won headlines
for Meher Baba the world over. The prospect of a
World War draws nearer every day, and most of us
now take it for granted. It needs no prophet to
foresee the inevitable, but it is important to
remember that Meher Baba has been predicting it for
years now, from immediately after the last armistice
when another such war seemed impossible. The next
war, according to Meher Baba, will be shorter, but
far more terrible than the last, and India will be
radically affected; and as a result of it, social and
economic conditions in this country will be
revolutionized. The last war was not enough to bring
about a change of heart in man, says Meher Baba,

and to this statement all can agree. The world purged of its pride will listen to reason only after an even more terrible purgatory.

" 'That is your opinion then,' I continued; but Meher Baba looked straight at me and smiled, while His fingers traced out on the cardboard:

'My son, I have no opinion to offer. I know.' "

Excerpt from "Notes from My Diary"
An Interview and Explanation on "Perfection"
by F. H. Dadachanji

During one of the rare interviews given by Meher Baba in Jubbulpore in 1938, the important subject of "Perfection" was discussed, and Baba gave an interesting explanation.

"Just as everything in the domain of duality is based on the proportion of degrees, so also is perfection based on degrees when concerned with duality. Bad and good, vice and virtue, weakness and strength are all based on degrees when considered with duality. Bad and good, vice and virtue, weakness and strength are all aspects of duality, but in reality it is unity of degrees. Bad is not bad but good in its lowest degree; so is weakness not weakness but strength in its lowest degree. Perfection has also its degrees when compared with imperfection. So you will find one perfection not including every perfection when in duality. One man perfect in science won't be found perfect in singing; and one perfect in singing won't be found perfect in painting. So these perfections are under the domain of duality.

"Have you ever heard of perfect crimes? When murder is so cleverly perpetrated as not to leave a single clue behind, it is called a perfect crime. So even in crimes and so-called sins, there is perfection.

"Now the perfection attained by spiritually perfect souls is not in the domain of duality. All these relative perfections, explained above, come within the scope of intellect, but the perfection of spiritually perfect souls is beyond intellect. When one is perfect spiritually, one knows that nothing exists except God alone; and so everything that exists under intellect and under the domain of duality is illusion to him. So for the perfect man, nothing exists but God. Science, art, music, weakness, murders are all dreams to him. His knowledge, his perfection is one indivisible existence.

"Now when this perfect soul, for spiritual reasons, wants to use all his power and knowledge, he does it purely for the sake of spiritual upliftment. Then he puts universal mind in that subject and knows all, even though the outward expression is not necessary, because all languages come first from the mental limit and are then expressed orally. But he knows the mind of everyone, so in any language, even before it is uttered, he knows the purport. So with everything—science, art, etc. If he wants, he can know even before it is manifested. But he does it only when necessary."

Question: Does Meher Baba believe in the theory of previous births as mentioned in the *Bhagavad Gita?*

Answer: **"Yes, it is all on the law of reincarnation that existence is based."**

Question: Lord Krishna was materially perfect too—so are you also not perfect materially?

Answer: **"That includes all perfections, but there is no need of expression. Krishna was perfect spiritually. That means he was perfect in everything, but he never expressed the material side of perfection, as there would be no meaning of perfection and because it would be all confusion. He could have shown himself a perfect drunkard, a** perfect sinner, a perfect rogue, but that would have shocked the world. So he didn't express it. So he was a perfect drunkard, perfect sinner, perfect rogue, perfect in everything—must have been—and a perfect God—above all."

Question: But was it necessary for him to show himself a perfect murderer?

Answer: "So I said—when it is necessary, these perfect souls express their perfection in everything. I can be perfect in any mode of life I have to adopt for the need of spiritual upliftment, and not merely to show perfection. Perfection when in its highest form includes every aspect—Sansar perfect, yoga perfect—perfect attachment, perfect detachment."

Excerpt from
"Notes from My Diary"

by F. H. Dadachanji

We give below some of the interesting questions
Meher Baba answered during interviews at the
"Links," Bangalore, in 1938.

Question: What is true spirituality?

Meher Baba: "**Spirituality truly means the life of
the spirit. It is to be lived and experienced. It makes
you firm like a rock and neither worldly sorrows
nor pleasures upset you. You attain to the state
where desires end and you want nothing. When you
do not want anything, you have everything. Look at
this mast (Chatti Baba). He is so innocent, always so
happy and so loving—for the simple reason that he
wants nothing; and strange as it may seem he has
everything—happiness, eternal peace of mind and
contentment.**

"**The state of desirelessness or of wanting
nothing is a faculty latent in everyone. It is within
you and you must find it out. I have found it and
experienced it. I know that everyone has this
faculty, but being latent it has to be found and
experienced. The difference between you and Me is
that although this faculty in Me is also present
within you, I have actually experienced and felt it,
while you have yet to experience it and feel it. I see
Myself in you all as palpably as you see all these
material things with your eyes. It is a fact for Me.**

"**With your eyes you see everything external. At
the back of this external aspect there is not mere**

hollowness or spacelessness, but also pure nothingness. When you realize this pure nothingness you see how it has come out of everything which is in you. When this experience is gained, the faculty of wanting nothing is developed and you begin to experience it."

Question: How could a confirmed sinner be redeemed?

Meher Baba: "From my point of view none is so bad as not to improve and become good. Everyone, however depraved, can improve and become better till he becomes the best example for mankind. There is always hope for everyone."

Meher Baba at Bangalore, India, 1939.

MEHER BABA JOURNAL
February 1939

Excerpt from
"Notes from My Diary"
by F. H. Dadachanji

At the close of the year 1938, Meher Baba spent three days at Mandla, a quiet place about sixty miles from Jubbulpore situated at the junction of two great rivers of India, the Narbada and the Godavari. Baba had long since expressed His predilection for Mandla due to its spiritual atmosphere. It is here, He explained, that in ancient times lived great souls and saintly beings, *tapasvis* and yogis, ascetics practicing penances. One of the most inspiring incidents during the short stay at Mandla was the walk to the famous Sahasra-dhara (thousand waterfalls). Here, it is said, the river Narbada has its source. In the solitude of nature here stands the temple of the Perfect Master, Sankaracharya, who lived in these surroundings about twelve hundred years ago. At the river bank Meher Baba performed the symbolic action of putting His foot into the river, explaining the significance of this gesture by saying that wherever the Avatar touches a river with His feet, the waters are purified for all those who come after.

. . . In one of His pensive moods, Meher Baba one day gave a discourse on general subjects and in particular on the benefits of Guru-Sahavas (contact with a Master). He also touched on a very important point, the elimination of the ego: **"The three most important things to be eliminated before attaining God-realization are greed, lust and ninda; the last,** meaning 'back-biting,' is the worst and most disastrous. One can overcome greed, or even lust, though both of these are very hard to get over; but the worst and most difficult of all to eliminate is this habit of ninda: speaking ill and trying to find faults or flaws in others; because this particular act or vice incurs the burden of sins or what is technically termed as sanskaras of others."

. . . Meher Baba and His party left Jubbulpore on the 15th of January for Benares via Katni. A representative of the Associated Press in Jubbulpore sought Meher Baba for a message and also wished certain questions answered.

Question: How long will the present chaotic state of affairs continue in the world?

Answer: **"As long as selfishness exists as its root cause."**

Question: How long will your Holiness stay in Jubbulpore in particular and India in general?

Answer: **"I leave Jubbulpore on the 15th, continuing my tour to Benares, Agra, Ajmer, Kashmir and other places, and intend to return to Jubbulpore in April. I intend to open a spiritual center here or at Mandla."**

Question: What is your Holiness's opinion about Mahatma Gandhi?

Answer: **"He is a good, noble soul, trying to serve humanity with all his heart."**

Question: When does your Holiness think India will be liberated?

Answer: **"When Hindus and Mohammedans cease quarreling."**

Question: Will the Jews, the most oppressed nation in the world at present, be able to withstand the onslaught that is being perpetrated on them by Hitler and Mussolini?

Answer: **"Jews or no Jews, whosoever sticks to**

truth or is on the side of truth can withstand any onslaught."

Question: Will your Holiness kindly give me a Message which I may broadcast to the world?

Meher Baba's Message
9th January 1939

"When suffering leads to real eternal happiness, we should not attach importance to this suffering. It is to eliminate suffering that suffering has to come.

"People suffer because they are not satisfied; they want more and more. Ignorance gives rise to greed and vanity. If you want nothing, would you then suffer? But you do want. If you did not want anything, you would not suffer even in the jaws of a lion.

"The widespread dissatisfaction in modern life is due to the gulf between theory and practice; between the ideal and its realization on earth. The spiritual and material aspects of life are widely separated instead of being closely united. There is no fundamental opposition between spirit and matter, or, if you like, between life and form. The apparent opposition is due to wrong thinking, to ignorance.

"The best and also the easiest way of overcoming the ego and attaining divine consciousness is to develop love and to render selfless service to all humanity in whatever circumstances we may be placed. All ethics and religious practices lead to this. The more we live for others and the less we live for ourselves, the more the lower desires are eliminated; and this in turn reacts upon the ego, suppressing it and transforming it proportionately.

"The root of all our difficulties, individual and social, is self-interest.

Meher Baba feeding fish at Mandla, India.

"Eliminate self-interest and you will solve all your problems, individual and social.

"The world will soon realize that neither cults, creeds, dogmas, religious ceremonies, lectures and sermons, on the one hand, nor on the other hand ardent seeking for material or physical pleasures, can ever bring about real happiness; only selfless love and universal brotherhood can do it."

Excerpt from
"Notes from My Diary"
by F. H. Dadachanji

On the 18th of March 1939 Mr. K, a great Congress worker, visited Meher Baba and had a conversation with Him of general interest. When Mr. K. was introduced to Meher Baba, it was explained that he was an Indian civil servant and held responsible government posts, but gave it all up for service to the country through Congress. Meher Baba thereupon remarked with regard to the spirit of true sacrifice:

"Sacrifice is sweet when it is for a good cause."

Question: Is faith in God essential?

Answer: "That depends on how you interpret faith. Some who have faith and believe in God lead a life without character and fail to make any spiritual progress; while there are others who do not even believe in God but lead such a noble life that they automatically come closer to God."

Question: What is the goal of creation?

Answer: "To know the Self as the infinite eternal existence and to enable others to realize this same Self."

Question: How did the Universe come about?

Answer: "This needs long explanation. Universe, if understood as created, has an entirely different meaning from our viewpoint that universe does not exist. Actually it is only God who appears as universe. But it is necessary to creation to have this dual idea of God and universe.

"To know the exact meaning of the 'awake' state, one has to experience the 'dream' state. Dreams can be good and bad. In dreams you can suffer or enjoy. But when you wake up you find it is all a dream. But this dream should be so adjusted that it awakens you soon. Sacrifice, character and selfless service help in waking you soon."

Question: Why do forces of evil predominate over forces of virtue?

Answer: "It is all in the scope of universal law. The suffering that appears so grave is necessary for happiness, as binding is necessary to experience freedom. Unless evil temporarily triumphs, suffering cannot be experienced. This universe is based on duality. Binding and freedom, bad and good, evil and virtue are interdependent. If only one aspect existed, there would be no meaning or interest in life. For the attainment of ultimate freedom and happiness, temporary victory of evil over virtue is necessary."

Question: Why does God, who is so kind and merciful, give suffering and pain to so many?

Answer: "God has nothing to do with this. God is all one-in-one. He is aloof and yet so attached that whatever is done is by His law of love and will. For example, when you sleep you enjoy a dream, and the enjoyment is so intense that this dream of happiness does not wake you soon. But if in the midst of the dream you suddenly saw a snake, you would at once wake up. This is the law of God. God is neither merciful nor cruel in your 'awakened' state."

Question: Is renunciation of the world necessary for spiritual attainment?

Answer: "Internal renunciation is necessary, but not external renunciation. It is not the outward escape from the world that leads you to God. You have to live in the world, do all your duties, and yet feel as detached as if you were living in seclusion in the midst of intense activity. How can you renounce this body and mind by retiring into the jungles?"

Question: In a slavish country like India, is it not the duty of every Indian to work for the liberation of his country?

Answer: "Yes, but the aspect must be from a spiritual standpoint. If material freedom binds you to Maya and leads to spiritual avoidance, it is no freedom. You must try heart and soul to have India free, but it must be the freedom that helps you towards truth and spirituality."

Question: Will India come in the forefront, as in the days of old, to lead the world?

Answer: "It is the duty of India to lead the world spiritually."

Question: Is the path shown by Gandhiji the only path to attain India's freedom?

Answer: "In some respects it is. It depends on the circumstances. If India were not so disunited internally as it is now, the policy of Mr. Gandhi would bring freedom in a few moments; but it is so difficult for the Hindus and Mohammedans to unite. Mr. Gandhi saw me four times and I said the same thing to him: that unless the hearts of Hindus and Mohammedans are united, little progress can be expected.

"Work with all your heart, with the one motive of making India truly free; but do not think of the results of your work. Men like you can do what millions cannot do, as you have heart, intellect and sincerity. This selfless service of yours in striving for India's freedom will lead you ultimately to God."

Excerpt from "Meher Baba and His Mad-Masts"

by Dr. C. D. Deshmukh

Those who would grasp the real significance of Meher Baba's work in connection with the Mad-Masts must always keep in mind that most of the Mad-Masts whom He has been attending to are of an extraordinary type. The Mad-Masts must not be confused with ordinary mad persons in whom there has been insufficient development of mentality. There are many mental hospitals all over the world which seek to give psychic and medical help to the febbleminded and to the mentally ill; and this in itself constitutes one of the most noble activities which in modern civilization has sprung out of philanthropic motives. But the work of Meher Baba in connection with his Mad-Masts is fundamentally different from this philanthropic work.

Meher Baba has Himself pointed out the differences between the Mad-Masts and ordinary mad persons. He gave this explanation: "**The Mad-Masts are God-mad. They are different from ordinary mad persons in respect to (1) the nature of their mental states; (2) the methods which are followed in the respective fields; and (3) the spiritual value of the results secured through healing. These important points of difference each need individual consideration.**

"**Differences in the origin of psychic disturbance: Persons who find shelter in the mental** hospitals are usually those who have either insufficient mental development or those who have lost their balance of mind due to the operation of physiological or psychic forces of disruption. These physiological or psychic forces which cause mental disturbances are of the ordinary kind. In such cases, the collapse of the normal functioning of the mind has come about by unmanageable conflicts or disintegrating factors; and the best that can be hoped for by removing the causes of disturbance is the restoration of normality to the mind. But the cases of the Mad-Masts are altogether different in their origin as well as in their potentiality. The Mad-Masts often exhibit incapacity to attend to and deal with the ordinary situations of life and are in this respect comparable to those who are deranged in mind; but their departure from normal behavior and responses is not due to lack of sufficient development or any chaotic forces of disruption, but is due to the suspension of interest from the ordinary pursuits of life and absorption in the spiritual realities encountered on the path towards God-realization.

"From the purely theoretical point of view, even these cases could be shown as cases of mental conflicts; but ordinary mental derangement is due to acute and insoluble conflict between incompatible sanskaras in connection with the world; whereas the unusual psychic states of the Mad-Masts are due to the dispersion of sanskaras by the powerful urge to realize God-states. The advancing urge to realize the highest brings about the shattering of the given mental structure with all its normal tendencies and corresponding capacities; and this condition of inhibited mind is called Unmani state. The successful termination of this urge initiates the aspirant into the supra-mental state of integral understanding and direct realization of the supreme self.

"Differences in the method of healing: In the case of ordinary mad persons the usual methods of cure consist in counteracting the physiological causes that might have contributed to the mental trouble. In the case of mental trouble of psychic origin the patient might be separated from the circumstances which led to his trouble, and sometimes, through the expert help of analysts, enabled to bring to the surface the complexes and the conflicts which he was reluctant to face and solve and which eventually brought about the disruption of his mental processes. But the analyst cannot give him the power to solve these problems; and the patient has to depend upon such power as may be immediately available to him. The part played by gentleness in the treatment of the analyst is considerable; but even with all the gentleness which he may command, the analyst is often unable to achieve success owing to lack of capacity to arouse the latent powers of the patient. An ordinary analyst who has little insight into spiritual realities can hardly be expected to help the Mad-Masts whose experiences and objectives are entirely beyond the range of his imagination. Only a Perfect Master can give them the help that they badly need; for He sees through their spiritual yearnings and peculiar obstacles and is also able to push them forward towards the goal or bring them back to normality, through the use of occult methods and by bringing to bear upon them consummate understanding, Divine Love and unfailing patience.

"Differences in the spiritual value of emergent states of consciousness: During this process of transcending the mind, the make-up of the mind is subjected to so much disturbance that the person is unable to use his mind in the ordinary way and to all appearances is like a mad man. Very often common people actually take him to be insane; but the Masters who have direct and real insight into the working of his mind know the true genesis and the nature of his unusual mental state and they are in a position to understand his condition in terms of spiritual values and to help him towards the realization of the goal which he is seeking in his own way. When these persons receive the right sort of help from a Perfect Master they emerge into a supranormal state of perfect integration and harmony.

"The Mad-Masts are God-intoxicated souls who in the joy of their advancing sojourn through the inner planes often lose their balance of mind; but this lost balance is in the end fully and finally re-established when the obstructive factors in the journey are all overcome. As compared with the normal man, the Mad-Masts seem to have less balance; but it is important to remember that the normal man does not have true or lasting balance and has only an appearance of balance, because he can successfully strike a provisional compromise between the warring elements in his psyche and can bring his outward behavior into conformity with the established conventions of society. But in order that the mind should arrive at the true balance of understanding, the provisional balance of compromise has to be considerably disturbed; and this is what happens in the case of the Mad-Masts.

"However, in spite of the fact that many of the Mad-Masts do actually lose their balance while traversing the spiritual path of inner life, they are often capable of rendering effective service to other aspirants who are less advanced than themselves. Though oblivious of worldly considerations and values, they are sensitive to the spiritual needs of those who come in touch with them; and as some of them are consciously stationed on the higher planes, they can give just that type of occult help which is necessary. The Mad-Masts who are entirely absorbed in the 'beatific vision' are capable of being perfected through the divine help which they receive from the Master who knows all the stages of the journey with its traps and dangers; and after being perfected they become perfect vehicles of the expression of the divine will to carry on God's plan on earth."

Meher Baba's help to his Mad-Masts is unique. He lives on the plane of Unity and for Him there are no veils; and just as a child in its uttermost simplicity and unsophisticated outlook can come into perfect harmony with any surroundings, irrespective of the distinctions of convention, Meher Baba at once

Meher Baba washing masts at Rahuri, 1937.

succeeds in establishing perfect understanding with the Mad-Masts. His method of helping the Mad-Masts works wonders because He can go down to their level. He can thoroughly enter into their lives because of His selfless universality and outgoing love which does not falter at spontaneous service of the humblest type. He is found to cut their hair, bathe them, feed them, attend to their physical ailments and even clean up their latrines. While attending to the Mad-Masts He is so forgetful of Himself and identifies Himself with their real problems so completely that their souls immediately recognize the Master as the medium of divine intervention and dispensation and respond to Him. Meher Baba appeals to the deeper layers of the inner being of the Mad-Masts and evokes responses which are sure signs of the activation of hitherto untapped resources and the release of the inner fund of spiritual energy which was so far inaccessible to them.

Meher Baba with mast at Rahuri, 1937.

MEHER BABA JOURNAL
September 1940

Excerpt from "Notes from My Diary"
Peculiar Traits of Saints and Masts and the Dangers of Dissuading Them
by F.H. Dadachanji

One of the oldest inhabitants of the Master's mast-ashram, Mohammed, has a strange habit of gazing fixedly at an object, not for minutes but at times for hours; then picking it up to bring it into his room. He is so lost in it that the slightest disturbance from anyone annoys him. When asked what he is doing, he will say, even without lifting his eyes from the object in view, "*Deesh pahato*," meaning "I am looking at something I like or want." It may be anything—a blade of grass, a piece of paper, stone or even mud—anything lying on the ground that attracts his attention, where he fixes his gaze and seems to look for something. He is so much absorbed, rather lost in it, that he wouldn't mind being exposed to such elements as the hot sun, cold drafts or heavy showers.

Those who look after him have at these times the rather awkward duty of bringing him in under a roof for the sake of his health. It is awkward because any effort at diverting his attention literally hurts him and he naturally resents it. Force cannot be used, under orders from the Master, but if left alone he might catch cold or get sunstroke or suffer from anything that may affect his health. It is at such moments that one has to be very tactful in handling and persuading him, lovingly or with mild threats like those we give to little children; and it is in this that the greatest test of those serving the masts is made.

Those who have worked under a Master know that so long as things go on smoothly and as desired by the Master, His visits may be less vigilant. But the moment there is something amiss, before we have time to think of it or correct it, we see Him in our midst, asking questions about the very thing that has gone wrong. And then He straightens it out in His own way, at times sternly and with strictures, at times mildly and with love, as the exigencies demand; but always impressing upon all the necessity of obeying His orders literally to avoid pitfalls and dangers that the slightest divergence might bring. Here is a typical instance:

In Ranchi, Mohammed was once in his usual mood, standing in the open looking at what he calls his "deesh." It suddenly began to rain. He was called in, but he wouldn't move. When repeated calls had no effect, B., who was in charge of the masts, annoyed at Mohammed's resistance lest it affect his health, went out personally and, rebuking him for his refusal to listen and to come in, tried to pull him inside with his hands. This brought tears to Mohammed's eyes. The shower by this time had become heavier and even under the umbrella they were drenched.

To the surprise of all, Meher Baba, who had been on the other side of the bungalow, appeared instantaneously on the scene and demanded an explanation. Mohammed, in his childlike way and with tears still in his eyes, pleaded that he was looking at his deesh and B. forcibly pulled him out. B. argued that it was for Mohammed's health that he felt concerned and tried to bring him in, even forcibly. Both were right yet both were wrong. Mohammed could not be blamed, for reasons Baba knew best; and, as He explained clearly later, B. cannot be blamed for the rather harsh manner in which he tried to pull Mohammed, motivated as it was for his health.

We mandali welcome these incidents since they give us opportunities to learn something new from Baba, from the unique way in which He tackles these situations and at times gives us such splendid explanations. In this case He saw the necessity once and for all to explain clearly why these masts behave in the peculiar manner they do and why they should be tolerated rather than disturbed, even at the cost of other inconveniences, and the patience which their peculiar behavior demands.

Meher Baba's Explanation

"All the care you bestow and the food and clothing, etc., you give them is no obligation for them at all; for they do not need these. Rather they resent all these, and in allowing you an opportunity to serve them, they are obliging you. They are no ordinary mortals but true lovers of God who have lost themselves in His Love and attained the state of walis (saints). They have no other desire but of God, whose Divinity they have seen on the different stages of their progress. And they are dazed. They need a spiritual push from a Perfect Master. That is why I have them here, serving them Myself and giving you an opportunity to serve them. But being used to living freely and happily at their will and according to their peculiar whims and methods, it is a binding on them to live here; and, but for Me, they would not stay for a moment. To distract them from the particular thing in which they are interested and finding happiness is a torture to them. They find a sort of relief or happiness in staying in or even in

Meher Baba embracing the mast Mohammed, Meherabad, 1939.

playing with dust and dirt. They do not see in these their external form or appearance; but they see God's Divinity in these. Mohammed is always going out to find something on which to fix his gaze because he sees in that particular thing something which pleases him. That is his method and that is his trait.

"If you try to stop masts from doing certain things, even with the best intentions, to keep them clean and out of dust and dirt, they feel disturbed in the ecstasy they are enjoying through that medium and are naturally enraged. If in a fit of excitement they were to say something, you would be doomed for life. The wrath of some of these highly advanced masts who are saints is very dangerous.

"Saint Tukaram has explained this very clearly in one of his abhangas (sacred hymns): that you should beware of close contact with saints, as there is always the risk of one of their typical traits (characteristics), good or bad, sticking to you, and if this happens, there is no escape. These can even wipe off your best sanskaras of previous births. It is therefore better that you keep yourselves away from them. Even if you have a desire for their darshan and want to offer your prostrations, do that from a distance.

"One of the well-known Mohammedan saints had a peculiar trait. While passing along the road, even in a big city like Bombay, in one of his ecstatic moods he would all of a sudden stop in the middle of the road between the tram-lines and obstruct all traffic for minutes. People knew it and tolerated it and didn't disturb him until he walked out by himself.

"Mohammed's trait of finding and looking at his deesh is a sort of relief to him, to be thus occupied. You think that he is playing with dirt and exposed to the elements. With the best of motives of safeguarding his health you try to bring him in. When he resists, you forcibly try to pull him out and break his link of what he has seen in that particular object through the higher consciousness of the spiritual plane in which he is. And what happens? The moment he finds you trying to dissuade him, he feels disturbed and is indecisive whether to be there or here, i.e., where his consciousness has taken him on the higher planes through the thing he is looking at, or where he is called on by you to go, leaving his deesh on this earthly plane. And this is no joke. It is a regular torture to him to reconcile the two different and conflicting states of the higher and lower planes of consciousness. If in the torments of these tortures or excitement he were to abuse or curse anyone for thus disturbing him in the enjoyment of his ecstasy, the cursed one would be doomed for life. It is simply because of Me (Baba) that he cannot do this and you are saved.

"That is why I have been asking you constantly to be very tolerant and lenient with them and never to disturb them if they are persistent, even with the best of motives to protect them from the elements, etc., which is also one of your duties to look after. The best way to handle them is the way of love and mild persuasions. If these do not succeed, nothing else will. Compulsion or force would be worse, even if they cannot hurt you for My sake. It reacts on them and hurts them to suffer, which I do not want. For I know what a torture it is to them and how they suffer. It is a torture both ways. First of all, they suffer for being deprived of their own environment and freedom in the spots where they used to live, and to be thus kept confined, even with all the other liberties we give them and the best care we take of them. Secondly, they suffer when thus disturbed and pulled out of their ecstatic enjoyments. It is because they feel happy in My presence that they stay. They see Me and know Me as none of you do. That is why they are quiet. Otherwise they would be impossible to manage.

"If efforts made with love are effective with worldly people, they would be all the more effective and essential in dealing with these saintly beings who are lost in the love of God. You love to enjoy one phase of some of their peculiar traits when they are quiet and pleasing. You should equally enjoy the phase in which they insist on having the experience of the bliss they find in certain things which your eyes cannot penetrate nor your minds understand."

Excerpt from
"Notes from My Diary"
by F. H. Dadachanji

Meher Baba's seclusion continues, though partially relaxed. His stay at Meherabad, although apparently quiet, with no interviewing with visitors, is occupied with His internal work which proceeds with all the more intensity, as can be seen from the notable events that transpired during the period under review. These two months of December 1941 and January 1942 have been memorable and important.

During the month of December, Baba went out twice on tours to contact masts and spiritually advanced souls. The first trip was to Pandharpur, one of the most important places of pilgrimage in the Deccan. Miraj, Sangli and a few other places in that surrounding area were also visited to contact masts. The most important event was His second tour to Allahabad at the end of December, to contact 7,000 sadhus and advanced souls; this, as Baba explained, was meant to "give a final touch to this great work" that He has been doing since 1936.

To make preliminary arrangements for the arduous task of contacting 7,000 sadhus and masts at Allahabad, during one of the important fair festivals held about every twelve years, Pleader, one of the experts who had handled this work already, was sent to Allahabad ten days ahead. He set about it very energetically, undergoing great physical strain for days, and did it perfectly, as Baba remarked.

The members of the party selected by Baba to accompany Him and participate in this tour for the mast work were those who had at one time or another during all these years participated in this particular work in company with Baba.

On His return from Allahabad to Ahmednagar, Baba traveled by the Grand Trunk route, visiting Secunderabad and Sholapur, where He contacted masts during a few hours' stay.

A very important event that occurred during the month of December was the sudden passing away of Upasni Maharaj of Sakori, on the 24th. In a meeting of the mandali held on 26th morning at Meherabad, in the mast ashram on the hill, Meher Baba explained, among other things, that the breaking of His Silence will also be as sudden and unexpected as the passing away of Upasni Maharaj. The difference will, however, be in the general "feeling" which will be very strong when He speaks. All will feel it. It will shake the world like an earthquake. In different degrees will the different parts of the world and different people feel the shock.

In memory of the late Upasni Maharaj, Meher Baba specially ordered all the mandali staying with Him at Meherabad, and also at other places, to observe complete fast (without any meal and with tea twice only) on the 13th of January, 1942, which is the *Sankrant* day. Baba also ordered that a public bhandara (feast) be given the next day, the 14th of January, at Meherabad.

In accordance with Meher Baba's wish and instructions, His mandali staying at Meherabad and those at Bangalore, Nasik, Ahmednagar, Poona, Bombay, Karachi, Madras, Navsari and other places in India, and those abroad in Europe and in the

U.S.A. commence this year 1942 with the specific disciplinary orders of observing fast on one meal a day, and meditation, during the first month and a half—from January 1st till 15th February, 1942—to participate in His world work.

Meher Baba also expressed His wish that during this important period of a month and a half, simultaneously with His mandali, all others who can and want to should observe fast, taking only one meal a day. An announcement to this effect was published in a few leading papers of India: "In connection with His work for the spiritual upliftment of the world, Meher Baba has instructed His disciples and devotees in India and abroad to observe fast on one meal and twice tea every 24 hours, from the 1st of January 1942 to the 15th of February 1942. (Water to be taken freely.)

"Meher Baba would like *all others who can and want* to share in this work by observing fast as above."

Dhuni Festival

During the first week of January, Meher Baba ordered that the Meherabad dhuni (fire), which was lighted on the 12th of December for a day, be lighted again on January 12th, and this process be continued every month on the 12th for a day, until further orders.

Only this month, in memory of the late Upasni Maharaj, this dhuni should be kept burning for 48 hours, instead of 24 as was to be done every other month.

Baba arrived a few minutes before 7 p.m. on Monday January 12th at the dhuni by the neem tree under which His seclusion cabin is located. He looked at the photos of Upasni Maharaj and Himself placed near the dhuni, and then sat on a wicker chair after being garlanded by B.D. Jessawalla—known among

Baba's mandali as "Papa." Baba sat facing the west, while those mandali present at Meherabad stood round the specially prepared ground. When Baba gave the signal, Papa Jessawalla lit the fire, and at Baba's order all those present then placed some sticks of sandalwood on the fire. As soon as the fire was thus burning well, Baba made a few remarks.

Mohammed the Mast

On the 9th of January, Mohammed, the old favorite of the mast ashram and one of the most important mediums of Baba's mast work, was brought back to Meherabad for a casual meeting with Baba for a few hours and then sent away immediately. Although he had stayed with Baba for years and was also taken by Baba to the West, he had been sent away by Baba after His work was over. The improvement in his mental condition could be judged from the fact that he could recognize every member of the mandali whom he saw now at Meherabad after an absence of nearly a year. This shows the great contrast to his spiritually dazed condition when he first came to Baba and remained asleep *in the same position* without food and water for four days consecutively. It also speaks of a wonderful change that Baba brings about in souls who have lost consciousness in their independent pursuit of God.

Ending of the Year—1941; A Retrospect

Summarizing the important events that recently transpired during the last period of the year 1941 that has just ended, things seem to have happened, as foretold by Meher Baba to His mandali, in regular sequence. Let us have a retrospect. We can find: 1. The conflagration of the European War covering a wider range and spreading from West to East and making it practically a World War, with the

U.S.A. and Japan falling in. 2. The second important event was the memorable meeting of the two Masters—the late Upasni Maharaj and Meher Baba—after 19 years. 3. The subsequent passing away of Upasni Maharaj just two months after the memorable meeting. 4. Last, but not the least, Meher Baba's giving an almost final touch to the mast work during His important tour to Allahabad, just during the last three days of the year 1941 and significantly ending on 31st of December—actually the last day of the year, as if to close that important chapter.

Meher Baba's Trip to Allahabad

Before terminating the seclusion, the fast and the extensive tours for contacting masts, Baba declared that He would touch 7,000 sadhus. This decision did not come as a surprise to some of Baba's old disciples, as some twenty years ago, while traveling in the Nilgiri hills, Baba had said that He would once contact 7,000 sadhus.

The Kumbh Mela of Allahabad is known to be India's greatest fair, where several lakhs of people assemble once every twelve years. The Kumbh Mela of 1941-42 has the additional significance of being known as the Maha Kumbh Mela, having a cycle of 36 years. The spiritual significance of Allahabad, where the Jumna and the mythical Saraswathi have their confluence with the Ganges, draws hundreds of thousands of sadhus to the Kumbh Mela from all parts of the country.

The significance of Meher Baba's selection of the Maha Kumbh Mela of 1942 for contacting the 7,000 sadhus at this turning point in the spiritual history of the world, immediately after the demise of Upasni Maharaj and just before terminating His period of seclusion, etc., will be obvious to those who know Baba.

The creation of opposition by Maya and the consequent material difficulties appearing in every phase of the spiritual work of Baba is well known to His disciples. They also know that the difficulties eventually disappear with the same certainty with which they appear. The trip to Allahabad was no exception to the rule. Immediately after Baba's decision to go to Allahabad to contact the sadhus, we read in the papers of the decision of the Government of India to cancel all special trains to Allahabad—an important and usual feature of the Kumbh Mela—on account of military requirements. Not only the specials were cancelled, but the ordinary number of trains had also to be reduced, as also the number of carriages in the remaining trains. A rush to get to the trains was therefore expected as a certainty, particularly on account of the evacuation of some of the eastern ports. We were confident that in spite of the difficulties Baba's work would be completed; but at the same time we were under no delusion about the troubles to be encountered.

Meher Baba decided to leave Meherabad on 29th December 1941 by the morning train. When we came to the station we were informed that the line was blocked by military specials and that it was not known when the passenger train would arrive at Ahmednagar; and that therefore we would not be able to get the Allahabad connecting train from Manmad. Soon we found ourselves driving with Baba on the Ahmednagar-Manmad road in a bus supplied by Sarosh Motor Works.

The road from Ahmednagar to Manmad passes some important spiritual centers, including the *Dargha* of Sai Baba; Sakori, the residence of Upasni Maharaj; and Dahigaon, where the meeting between Meher Baba and Upasni Maharaj took place. The question therefore which puzzled us was whether it was really an accident that we had to make this eleventh hour change, or whether it had deeper significance that Baba should go on His important spiritual mission crossing the spiritual atmosphere of Sakori and the surrounding country. As we were traveling in the bus, Baba pointed out to us the hut where He met Upasni Maharaj last. The quiet hut could be seen far away from the road.

The beautiful Ankai Hills, about ten miles from Manmad, are known to several disciples of Baba who have spent time in meditation there. As we came near the Ankai Hills, Baba called a halt for breakfast. All had enjoyed the memorable drive with Baba, and the rough road with the deep ruts and holes had added to the pleasure, while the bumps and jerks had made everybody all the more hungry. Baba sat near us under a huge banyan tree. A beautiful clear stream was flowing nearby and we had an excellent breakfast, then continued our journey and reached the station in time for the Allahabad train.

We arrived at Allahabad about ten o'clock in the morning on the 29th. After breakfast and a little rest at a hotel, Baba went out to the Kumbh Mela grounds with some of the members of the mandali. On reaching the grounds, we soon discovered that the work of touching the 7,000 sadhus was not going to be an easy task. It was hot and sultry, while the Mela ground was all sandy, and the sadhus were scattered throughout a radius of about two miles. Different schemes were suggested by the mandali for carrying out what seemed to be a herculean job; Baba did not approve any of the schemes. In fact, had He done so, several days would have been spent at Allahabad. Baba adopted His own scheme.

First of all, we had a reconnaissance round with Baba, which consisted of about four hours of strenuous walk in the loose sand and scorching sun.

During this rapid survey, we crossed the Ganges and the Jumna twice in a boat. While passing across the confluence of the Jumna and Ganges, Baba remarked that Allahabad is known for its spiritual atmosphere from days of old.

Having seen the place generally and deciding upon His program of work, Baba started the contacts with the sadhus. It was about sunset time when Baba touched the first sadhu. This sadhu, whom we encountered accidentally, as it were, when Baba decided to begin the contact work, was a very typical person. He was gazing straight at the setting sun and shouting loudly "Jap! Jap!" (Meditate! Meditate!) He was the only sadhu amongst the hundreds of thousands of them in the Kumbh Mela who had put on a typically mixed dress, partly Eastern style and partly Western. The long garment of the average Indian sadhu with some dirty torn clothes perhaps represented the East; while the old and shabby hat on his head was the probable pointer for the West. The question as to whether Baba selected this first sadhu accidentally, or whether the selection had a deep meaning, would provide an interesting study to the lovers of Baba's work of universal spiritual upliftment.

It is impossible to describe in words the second sadhu whom Meher Baba touched. Those who have read the life of Shri Chaitanya Maha Prabhoo, or have seen some of the pictures depicting his divine ecstasy, might be reminded of the condition of Shri Chaitanya when he was experiencing Divine Love and when he was dancing with lifted hands on the seashore at Jagannath Puri on seeing the visions of his beloved Krishna. To get some idea of the unforgettable scene we saw at Allahabad on 30th December 1941 at sunset, when Baba met the second sadhu at the Kumbh Mela, you have to substitute the sadhu in place of Shri Chaitanya and Baba in place of his beloved Krishna and the sandy bank of the Ganges in place of the Puri beach.

The sadhu—a young person about thirty years of age with a most handsome appearance and charming personality—saw Baba from a distance of some fifty paces, and for a while he danced with lifted hands as if he were in the happiest moment of his life. He walked a little and then sat down as if the feeling had overpowered him. Baba met him like the most loving mother embracing the dearest child. The sadhu was completely naked and his body was covered with dust and sand, but the way Baba was treating him showed that to Baba the apparently dirty body of the sadhu was of no consequence. Subsequently, when referring to this sadhu, Baba said he was a soul merged in the ocean of Divine Love. Baba further remarked: **"If someone were to ask me what makes me happiest, my reply would be 'embracing a mast' (a God-intoxicated soul) like the one you saw today."**

Referring to the value of the love of the marvelous sadhu, Baba said: **"Such love consumes the false ego and annihilates the lower self in the supra-conscious state wherein the highest asserts itself. Just as the state of man's communion with God, the soul's identification with the Oversoul and the lover's union with the Beloved are beyond the realm of understanding, so also is the state of this perfect lover of God indescribable."**

The second sadhu—a living Chaitanya Maha Prabhoo—had such attraction for Baba that in spite of the most strenuous labor He had to undergo the next day in contacting thousands of sadhus, Baba insisted on meeting this individual again, and spent about half an hour with him, in spite of the heavy pressure on His time.

On the first day, after acquainting Himself with the location of the sadhu camps, Meher Baba touched 359 sadhus. All of us were completely exhausted. Nobody, however, liked to say this and thus to interfere with Baba's work. To everybody's relief, Baba Himself said that He was tired and that the work would be resumed the next day. That in fact Baba was not really tired, and merely came to our rescue by saying so, became clear to us when, the next day, He arranged matters in such a way that while He had to move about constantly in the soft sand, we had to remain at specific places where He could easily communicate with us, while He moved about almost like a machine with inexhaustible energy.

He had not only to move about, but had also to bend down to touch the sadhus who were to be found in different postures. Some were lying on the ground, some were squatting, some were themselves moving about, while some were found in small huts with narrow, low doors. While we admired Baba's energy and power of endurance, we were growing more and more anxious about the after-effects of this herculean task on His health.

By the evening Baba had exceeded the figure of 7,000 in touching the sadhus. The actual hours of work were from about 6:00 in the morning to about 11:00 in the forenoon; and again from about 6:00 to 9:00 in the evening. The prayer time in the morning and evening selected by Baba helped Him considerably in doing the work quickly. Sadhus in groups of hundreds were found collected at different places for the prayers. Similarly at some of the big camps called the "Akhadas" of the sadhus, hundreds of them were found early in the morning. Again at the "Annachatras" (centers for distribution of free food to the sadhus) many of them were found in large numbers.

Baba was not idle between 11 a.m. and 6 p.m. on the 31st of December, the final day of the work of touching the sadhus. After late breakfast and about two hours rest, He took us to Naini, a place about five miles from Allahabad, to meet a mast. This mast had a charming personality and was known locally as Cha Sahib. We found him sitting on a cot inside a dark room where a fire was burning.

Baba had asked us to take with us tea in a large teapot, as Cha Sahib is exceedingly fond of tea. Seeing us at the door of the room, Cha Sahib got up from the bed and received us in a way that indicated he was expecting us and had known us for a long time. The sweet smile on his face, his sparkling lovely eyes and his lively gait showed that he was in the happiest of moods. He took the tea-pot from us and placed it on the fire and made us sit on his cot. He allotted a corner of the room away from us to Baba, and while pretending to talk to us generally about our health, and inviting us to have tea, he was all the while enjoying stealthy glances at Baba, who seemed to be so happy in the little dark corner of Cha Sahib's room. We again realized how Baba really feels so happy in the company of the masts. After spending about half an hour with Cha Sahib, Baba returned with us to Allahabad, where He went straight to the Mela grounds and completed the work of touching the 7,000 sadhus that evening.

On returning to the hotel at about 9 p.m., Baba had only a glass of ginger and then took a hot tub-bath before retiring to bed. With the strenuous work of the day, we were concerned about Baba's health, but He again gave us a surprise by getting up at five o'clock in the morning and feeling as fit as ever. His work having been completed to His satisfaction, Baba was in a very good mood, and after tea we left Allahabad by the Bombay Mail on the morning of the New Year, 1942.

Excerpt from
"A Prophet of the New Age"

by Charles J. Seymour
(London)

Meher Baba defines "spirituality" as: **"that which makes man more human. It is a positive attribute of realizing all that is good and noble and beautiful in man. It does not require the renunciation of worldly activities or the avoiding of duties and responsibilities. It only requires that while performing worldly activities or discharging responsibilities, the inner spirit should remain free from the burden of desires.**

"There is nothing irrational in true mysticism, when it is, as it should be, a vision of reality as it is. It is a form of perception which is absolutely unclouded; it is so practical that it can be lived every moment of life and can be expressed in everyday duties; and its connection with experience is so deep that in one sense it is the final understanding of all experience."

"Don't Worry"

by Delia de Leon

To be told by Meher Baba not to worry may seem a commonplace and simple thing. Those unaccustomed to His ways or newly meeting Him might wonder why He bothers to mention the obvious, for we all have our worries. Especially it might come as a shock to those who desire to hear from Him learned metaphysical or philosophical discussions. Meher Baba's concern is to awaken the love within us so that we may become real human beings. His appeal is to the heart. Directly and simply He gets down to the very roots of our being. Invariably He says:

"Don't worry; I will help you. Just love Me."

These words, like the words of Jesus,* are deep and significant; for they are a clarion call to us, to rouse ourselves, to awaken from our smug little outlook on life to yearn for a richer, fuller, deeper way of living.

If we want to understand Meher Baba's ways, we have only to pause and think a little to realize that the fundamental cause of most of the trouble that is shaking the foundations of our world today is worry, and its inevitable sister, fear. Everywhere we see entire nations and peoples in the grip of this worrying business. The life of the individual makes up the life and character of the nation, and each in

---

*"My peace I give unto you not as the world giveth, give I unto you. Let not your heart be troubled, neither let it be afraid." St. John, Chapter 14, Verse 27.

turn reacts on other peoples and nations. We worry because we lack health, possessions, money or lands. We poison our lives at the source and that affects our adjustments to each other. Then comes intolerance, greed and persecution. We have not got the right kind of faith—the faith that helps us recognize the rights and needs of all men to live peacefully in brotherhood and to know that we are all part of the whole. If we had this faith, we would know, as Hafiz says: "The object of all religion is alike—all men seek their Beloved. O, all the world is love's dwelling; why talk of a mosque or a church?"

Why do we worry so much? With many people it is because they feel an eternal dissatisfaction. They want things different; something eludes them always. Small wonder that in their desperate desire to be free from worry they follow false gods, thinking they will be led to Utopia. They are deceived by words and grandiose promises, and are "let down" invariably for they fail to realize that the remedy lies within themselves. It is only a Perfect One like Meher Baba that can give them the right answer to all that troubles them and the world today. He has Himself attained freedom and can help others to this freedom. If we turn to Him, He will help us and in Him we can find hope and strength. The very fact of His telling us **"Don't worry; be happy"** helps us and gives us power, for it loosens up within us the causes of our worries.

To love Him and to obey Him is the next step— it is so much easier with Him behind us. For it is a spiritual solution, and no amount of physical or mental striving can solve our problems. Meher Baba does help us to change our attitude to life; and it is not a negative attitude that Baba asks us to cultivate, but a positive, joyful acceptance of experiences in their right focus. Not to be caught up in the passing phases of illusion (Maya)—"to be in the world but not of it"—does not mean a shrinking from life. We have our parts to play. And to withdraw from life to practice austerities, to sit in a cave to meditate, does not necessarily mean spiritual advancement. It would not be right for the majority. Meher Baba seems to prefer us to be active and dynamic, though He wants us to accept whatever experience is necessary for our spiritual progress and development.

Meher Baba helps us in so many ways not to worry or fear and to develop this right attitude towards life. It sounds so simple yet most of us find it so difficult. **"Don't worry,"** says Baba to someone, and usually if that person is receptive he soon begins to realize what a worrier he is, even though it may have been in the depths of his subconscious self; and the measure of the new inrush of life that fills him is the measure of Baba's help.

It is a subtle and pernicious foe that we have to fight; but if we follow Baba's advice we soon find that troubles and fears begin to vanish, because the things that were important to us before do not matter any more. Why should we worry when we can turn to Him and love Him and serve Him?

We must try to know and understand ourselves truly; for Meher Baba says:

"Everything is within you: the secret of Life . . . God."

We are part of all; it is the veils of illusion that prevent our seeing clearly. We have gradually to shed these veils; to lose our ego, to die to the lower self; and we will awaken like a dreamer from sleep.

Sometimes Baba, in order to help us, brings our faults up to the boiling point. The person who worries, worries more than ever. A climax comes, an emotional upheaval takes place within the person. Then if they have the courage to face up to themselves, and to realize the fault lies within themselves, in a flash the whole thing clears up and they are free from that particular worry. If they lack courage or have not enough love or faith to trust Baba, then they perhaps turn against Him or blame Him for their own weaknesses.

Meher Baba is always there, waiting; ready to guide and teach us; whatever our weaknesses or worries, we can go to Him. And with patient love He will help us again and again.

Meher Baba's telling us not to worry has an added significance at the moment, for we are living in thrilling and trying times. The approaching spiritual age calls for our recognition of the verity of the brotherhood of man. All our resources and powers of endurance will be taxed in the struggle. Out of chaos, order comes. Meher Baba stands like a beacon, beckoning us on. He shows us by His example the heights we can reach; with perfect poise and equilibrium He walks the earth. His Love is our inspiration, and if there are dark days and all goes from us, we need not worry or despair.

Might He not be saying, as Francis Thompson says in *The Hound of Heaven:*

> *All which I took from thee,*
> *I did but take*
> *But just that thou mightest seek it in My arms.*
> *All which thy child's mistake*
> *Fancies is lost, I have stored up for thee at home.*
> *Rise, clasp My hands and come.*

Excerpt from "What Is Love?"

by Winifred A. Forster
(Hertfordshire)

"The true understanding of love is in the growth of consciousness of many of its various aspects as they open out to tender loving hearts that receive and respond and are ever eager to pass it on lovingly to others who need. Love is above all and always triumphs."

These words were written in a letter from the living Master of Truth, Meher Baba, whose supreme way is the way of Divine Love. The Master encourages and feeds what is already there. He does not impose anything from outside. It is all within, He insists. "The Kingdom of Heaven is within you" is re-expressed by the Avatar of today. He says:

"The Supreme Soul, God, is nowhere to be searched for. He is very near you; He is with you; seek Him within. God, the real Beloved, is ever ready to enter your house, the mind; but He cannot because it is occupied by your numberless unreal beloveds, your desires: and there is no room for Him."

When life has lost all meaning and all joy, it can become worth living for the sake of Love. Of what else can this be said? Love does ask us to have faith, however hard it is. Meher Baba understands that until the door of our heart is unlocked and fully opened, we still have doubts.

"One day you will see Me in there," He says, pointing to the heart. "And then all doubts will go." To one who despairs in life He says: "Your life is worth living now, for My Love. I do know, even if you do not. Remember, Love is above all and always triumphs."

Let us reassure ourselves that in spite of all we see in the world, Love has not abandoned humanity, and it is not doomed to perpetual darkness. The supreme exponent of Love is in our midst; the forces of light will prevail and overcome those of darkness. Let us have faith; Love alone can resurrect and Love alone is above all. "The whole creation groaneth and travaileth," and indeed it is true, but it is not for nothing. We cannot understand all at present, but we can trust in spite of all that the crucifixion of humanity is not its end, any more than the crucifixion of Christ ended His Love or His life. That life of Love is eternal, and upon it our life depends. Meher Baba says:

"When, from the depths of the heart, man desires something more lasting than wealth, something more real than material power, the wave of destruction will recede. Then peace will come, joy will come, light will come. The breaking of My silence—the signal for My public manifestation—is not far off. I bring the greatest treasure which it is possible for man to receive—a treasure which includes all other treasures, which will endure forever, which increases when shared with others. Be ready to receive it!"

SAYINGS
OF MEHER BABA

A man becomes wise by practicing, not by preaching virtue. Ability in advising others about virtue is no proof of saintliness, nor is it a mark of wisdom.

Do not get disheartened and alarmed when adversity, calamity, or misfortunes pour in upon you. Thank God, for He has thereby given you the opportunity of acquiring forbearance and fortitude. Those who have acquired the power of bearing with adversities can easily enter the spiritual path.

Pain and evil are real only in the sense in which dreams are real. Considered absolutely, only God is real; all other things, including pain and evil, are unreal.

The priest whose principal motive is to serve himself and not others should be called a minister not of God, but of his lower self. Disinterestedness and eagerness to serve others should be the characteristics of a genuine priest, to whatever creed he may belong. He should be like a river that does not drink its own waters, but is useful to others, irrespective of their caste, creed and color.

We cannot witness even the threshold of the divine path until we have conquered greed, anger and lust. The worst sinners are better than hypocritical saints.

You will not be saved by accepting any theological dogmas or by regarding a prophet who lived hundreds or thousands of years ago as the only God-incarnate, as the only genuine savior, as the last real messenger of God. If you want to be saved, conquer your mind, lead a pure life, renounce low desires, and follow one who has realized God and in whom you have sound faith.

Illusion is the basis of the juggler's tricks. Through Maya, the world, which is no more substantial than a mirage, appears to be real. Children admire the juggler and they think that his tricks are realities; but adults know that he is a trickster and that his tricks are illusion. Ignorant men regard the world as the ultimate reality, but Dnyanis [possessors of spiritual knowledge] know that it is only illusion.

One's guru must be spiritually more advanced than oneself—better if he is spiritually perfect. If you are in bonds and wish to be free, to whom should you go? Certainly to one who is quite free and not to one whose hands are tied. Similarly, if a person wishes that Maya should no longer bewitch him, he must go to one for whom Maya does not exist and who has completely subjugated his passions.

Humanity should be considered the greatest
test of civilization. He who is devoid of humanity
should be considered a barbarian. Though a man
may be very learned, very up-to-date in the worldly
routine of life, and advanced in scientific knowledge,
yet if he lacks humanity he is still a barbarian.

As a single object seems to multiply itself to
him who has drunk to excess, so unity appears as
plurality to those who are intoxicated with the wine
of egoism.

The so-called religious leaders who repeatedly
quarrel over rites and dogmas can only lead their
followers into the deep pit of ignorance. Only the
blind will follow the blind.
What light can be thrown by him who is
himself in the dark? What knowledge can he impart
who has not experienced truth?

Most of the so-called religious ceremonies
performed by the Parsees, the Hindus, and followers
of other creeds are unnecessary and worthless. For
these useless ceremonies it is the avaricious and
worldly priests who are responsible. Prophets,
Sadgurus, and saints are not bound by them.

Wearing the yellow robe, begging for bread,
visiting the holy places do not necessarily prove
sanyas or renunciation. The true sanyasin [spiritual
pilgrim] is he who has renounced his lower self and
all worldly desires.

169

It is praiseworthy to be a genuine sanyasin, but honest householders are far better than hypocritical sadhus. And today there are many false sadhus.

From the materialistic standpoint it may seem cowardly to forsake the world, but it requires great heroism to lead the spiritual life.

He who gets control over the mind gets everything under control.

If worldly desires and anger take hold of your mind, then no matter how much you may practice tapa-yapa and meditation, you are still entangled in the toils of Maya. Maya is the source of all worries, anxieties and troubles.

The limited 'I' bears at every stage the marks of change and conflict; but it strives for indivisible completeness of being.

All value truly and ultimately belongs to the Self and to the Self alone.

Section Three

Questions Meher Baba Answers

Meher Baba with young Indian child, Meherabad, 1938.

Questions Meher Baba Answers*

Series by Dr. Abdul Ghani Munsiff

April 1940

Question: What is the difference between destiny
and chance?

Answer: **"Destiny is the Divine law which
guides us through our numerous existences. Every
soul must experience happiness and unhappiness,
vice and virtue, from the commencement of
evolution up to that goal which is the realization of
God.**

**"Chance is based on karma, that law of cause
and effect which governs the events of our present
life as well as those of our future lives. Through
evolution the soul receives by means of the spirit
the impressions or sanskaras. The processes which
create the experiences, and later the elimination of
these impressions, can be called chance. Destiny or
the goal that souls have to attain is realization of
God; but actually chance is different for every
individual. We can compare destiny to a load of (let
us imagine) seven hundred tons of happiness and
unhappiness, vice and virtue, which every soul has
to carry throughout its existence. One soul carries
seven hundred tons of iron, another soul the same
weight in steel, others lead or gold; the weight is
always the same. Only matter changes. The
impressions of each individual vary and the acquired**

---

*These Questions and Answers have appeared in the French edition of
Questions and Answers (Paris).

sanskaras form the structure and condition of the future life of every individual."

Question: What is the difference between the exterior and interior work of the Avatar?

Answer: "His interior work is executed for the good of humanity by the means of his spiritual body and Divine will—on the spiritual and the subtle planes directly, or through the intermediary of His agents. The exterior work is accomplished through His physical body by personal contact with individuals. By passing through different countries He turns their minds towards spirituality; He enhances their progression towards the subtle planes and from these towards the spiritual planes."

Question: Why were certain Avatars married and why was Jesus not married?

Answer: "The exterior way of living of the Avatar is regulated by the habits and customs of the times, and He adopts that attitude which is most suited to serve as an example to His contemporaries. But in essence all the Avatars incarnate the same ideal of life. At the epoch of Mohammed the Arabs were very sensuous and it was not considered bad or illegal to live with several wives. If, like Jesus, He had not married and had advocated celibacy, or if He had imposed absolute continency, it would have produced dangerous and inevitable reactions. Few people would have followed His teaching and fewer still would have been attracted toward such an ideal. Mohammed had nine wives but He had no physical contact with them; it was legal to have several wives.

"At the time of Krishna the Hindus were fighting among themselves. Envy and greed were predominant; the real conception of spiritual life and love was unknown to them. Krishna based His teachings on the laws of love and pure and innocent merriment. Human beings were directed joyfully towards a disinterested ideal of love.

"At the time of Zoroaster humanity was hesitant and lacked equilibrium. They were neither complete materialists nor really attracted towards the spiritual light. He taught them to be good householders, to marry and to abstain from desiring the wife of another, and to worship God. His own life was based on this principle: good thoughts, good words, good actions. Zoroaster was married.

"At the time of Buddha, humanity was deep in materialism. In order to demonstrate that their conception of values was wrong and that they were victims of the goddess Illusion, or Maya, Buddha renounced his wife, his family, the riches of the world in order to establish His teachings on sanyas, or renouncement.

"At the time of Jesus, arrogance, imperiousness, pride and cruelty were the characteristics of the people. Nevertheless they possessed a conception of justice regarding women and marriage; and it was not necessary, as it was in Arabia, to make marriage an example. Jesus lived the life of humanity, simplicity and poverty; and He endured suffering in order to direct humanity towards the purest ideal— God. All the prophets were the incarnation of God; therefore they stand beyond desire and temptations; they were the manifestation of the same Divine element."

May 1940

Question: Why do the Avatars differ from one another in their teachings?

Answer: **"The Avatars are the manifestation of the same Divine element incarnate in this world at different times; therefore their teachings have to be** adapted to the mentality of their epoch. At times the Avatar bases His teaching on the search for the personal God; and at another time on the search for the impersonal aspect of God. At one time He will prohibit the eating of pig's meat, drinking of wine, or the eating of cow's meat. It is as in a hospital where the sick complain about their thirst: The doctor will prescribe tea or coffee in the morning, water or a refreshing fruit juice in the afternoon and in the evening sour milk; then before sleeping, hot milk. God, manifesting through the Avatar of different periods, quenches the thirst of man in different ways. All human beings, whether consciously or unconsciously, have the same thirst for truth."

Question: What does Meher Baba think about life after death?

Answer: "The semi-subtle sphere is the chain that links the physical, material world to the subtle plane. During our habitual dreams we make use of the subtle body and in a subconscious way we perceive sensations belonging to the physical, material world. In certain conditions it is possible to make conscious use of the physical senses in such a way that we can contact the semi-subtle sphere. We can, because of this fact, enter into communication with the spirits of the dead. These spirit communications have nothing to do with the spiritual life, nor with subtle spirit, nor with the spiritual planes. There is a vast difference between the subtle sphere and the semi-subtle sphere.

"After death the spirits of human beings (except for those who have sufficiently progressed on the spiritual path and are beyond the fourth plane) reach the semi-subtle sphere. According to their sanskaras they go to 'heaven' or 'hell'; and when they achieve the point they had to attain, they can return to earth

with a new body (reincarnate); or otherwise they
return to the semi-subtle sphere for a certain time.
These spirits are, so to say, in the ante-chamber of
the semi-subtle sphere and one can enter into
contact with them through the means of spirit
communication, whether they have achieved their
period of joy or pain, and wait for a new rebirth, or
whether they are on the point of going to 'heaven'
or 'hell.' The semi-subtle sphere, 'heaven' or 'hell'
with their respective experiences, have no reality.

*Meher Baba in front of The Dome at Meherabad, 1938, with mother
Shirinmai, brothers Adi, Jr., Behram and Jal, and sister Mani.*

They are merely joys and pains experienced through the organs of the subtle body.

"It is advisable to attribute only relative importance to certain descriptions of life after death, although they may be exact. Spiritually evolved persons can communicate with high spirits but it is preferable that they abstain. Human beings can never enter into communication with the high spirits who belong to the subtle, mental or spiritual planes; because even if they have to reincarnate they do not sojourn in the ante-chamber of the semi-subtle sphere."

March 1939

Question: In the presence of a spiritual Master, what is the propriety and significance of worldly activities, such as schools, hospitals, asylums, etc., which already are numerous in the world?

Answer: "It is true that the world abounds in similar institutions; but they are invariably philanthropically inspired. Institutions under My care have a spiritual purpose to serve. Worldly benefactions are demanded and created solely by society. My activities are nothing if not an objective manifestation of the Divine dispensation which sustains the phenomenal world. Divine wisdom, full of love and compassion, has been known to incarnate from time to time in answer to the call of humanity when it is faced with hopeless, unredeemable bankruptcy in all departments of life—moral, material and spiritual.

"For eyes that can discern, clearly unmistakable signs of disintegration, social and economical, usually preceding the advent of Divine manifestation, are in evidence all around.

Rehabilitation of the world morally and spiritually, with the automatic readjustment of economic and social structure, is the avowed mission of Divine manifestation on earth.

"To achieve this, universal mind with infinite consciousness does universal work in infinite ways. Whatever objective work is done by One of universal mind and infinite consciousness affects the whole scope of His working. If He fasts, the result of fasting is felt by the whole universe spiritually; if He observes silence, characteristic spiritual benefit accrues to the universe. Just as fasting and silence by an individual results in spiritual gain to the individual concerned, likewise fasting and silence by One of universal mind and infinite consciousness amounts to an ordeal or penance suffered by the universe itself, resulting in spiritual betterment of the whole.

"Besides moral and spiritual disruption, the world today is experiencing terrible economic chaos. To invite or to tempt the world to things spiritual, the material needs (individual or collective) must be satisfied before the mind can dispassionately accept the spiritual. When I give food and clothing with My own hands, it will result in the world gaining its economic and material welfare.

"When I wash the God-mad and the lepers, the effect will be that those of sub-normal or abnormal consciousness will be restored to normal or sub-normal consciousness; while the lepers will either be cured or their future embodiments will be considerably minimized.

"Accept it as a spiritual fact that every living spiritual Master, charged with duty, affects His surroundings according to the scope of His work. As the Master, so the atmosphere around."

April 1939

Question: Is the "consciousness" we are aware of in the human form the same in all the spiritual planes?

Answer: **"The unfoldment of consciousness in the lower evolutionary stages, mineral, vegetable and animal, is perfected in the human form. The consciousness you have now in the human form**

Meher Baba with Kaka at Meherabad, 1939.

continues the same throughout all the spiritual planes—the subtle, mental and supra-mental. There is this difference. In the lower evolutionary process culminating in the human, the consciousness at various stages differs in point of degree. It is a continuous process of unfoldment, always progressive, resulting in the full and complete consciousness of the human form. In the planes, however, the perfected consciousness of the human remains the same, but its scope or field of play becomes greatly extended.

"For instance: you are now conscious only of the gross plane; the subtle and mental worlds you are not aware of. Likewise, one in the subtle plane has consciousness of the subtle world only and is not conscious of the gross and the mental; also one in the mental plane has the consciousness of the mental plane only and is not aware of the gross or the subtle; one in the seventh plane—the supramental, the plane of perfection—has consciousness of all the planes: the mental, the subtle and the gross.

"You can thus see the consciousness of the human form continues throughout; and the field of play varies not in degree but in depth and extensiveness. In evolution there is a definitely determinable difference in the various stages of consciousness which is an incessant and persistent state of unfoldment resulting in the all-complete consciousness of the human form. In the higher planes, although this consciousness remains the same, there is an infinite difference between the consciousness of the subtle and mental, mental and supramental. This difference is sharp and defined, as there is no point of fusion or expansion as that which existed when consciousness was unfolding. It is on this account that one in the subtle plane identifies himself with that plane and deems this consciousness to be Perfection. Similarly, one in the mental plane identifies himself with the mental plane and the consciousness hereof is considered as Perfection. It is not Perfection at all; it is an illusion, rather self-delusion.

"You can now understand why one gets stuck in the plane where one is. It is extremely difficult for one to step into the mental plane from the subtle. It is impossible for one to go from the mental into the supramental unless helped by a Master.

"There is as much difference between the consciousness (in extensiveness) of the sixth and seventh plane as that between an ant and a human being. The seventh plane connotes Perfection; here one becomes consciousness itself."

October 1939

Question: How does Tawajjuh (concentration of the spiritual force) of a spiritual Master function? There are numerous instances of Sufi saints giving Tawajjuh to an aspirant of the Path. Do you ever give Tawajjuh? If so, when and how?

Answer: "**Tawajjuh in Sufism is the focussing of the spiritual force by a saint onto the disciple concerned. The current is usually directed to the first of the seven centers of spirituality in the human body, and this is generally admitted to be the heart of man.**

"This concentration of the spiritual current onto the heart of the disciple should not be mixed up with hypnotic suggestion. In hypnosis the mind of the subject becomes inert and passive. It is held in subjugation for the time being by the stronger mind of the hypnotizer. In this business, however, there is not a tinge of spirituality imparted or received.

"Differentiated from this, Tawajjuh is purely a spiritual operation which is helpful in rousing the latent spark of divinity already in man, and it is infrequently indulged in by saints only.

"There are different methods of imparting Tawajjuh; but the most important are: 1. Islahi (corrective concentration); 2. Alqai (subtle or psychic); 3. Ittehadi (unifying); 4. Qalabi (spiritual).

"1. The Islahi Tawajjuh (corrective influence) of the spiritual Master cleanses the heart of the disciple of all mundane desires. The disciple in course of time becomes more tolerant in outlook, less conservative in ideas and beliefs, and generally settles down into an attitude of 'live and let live.' In short, the temporary feeling of disgust towards the unfavorable circumstances of the world (defeatism) gradually crystallizes into a spirit of complete renunciation and self abnegation.

"2. The Alqai Tawajjuh (psychic concentration) is the next higher step, and is brought into operation when the mind of the disciple is completely purged of all things foreign to it. Under its influence the heart is so very perfectly attuned that it receives instructions and guidance regarding the difficulties and the subtleties of the spiritual path direct from the Master, whose physical presence or absence makes no difference whatsoever.

"3. Ittehadi Tawajjuh (unifying concentration) is a phenomenon very rarely to be witnessed. This Tawajjuh, if given, results in a complete metamorphosis of the disciple, both spiritual and physical. Here the disciple not only becomes spiritually alike unto the Master, but even physically, as a result of sudden metabolical changes, he becomes an exact replica of the Master's physical form.

"One such instance is on record with regard to

the Master Khwaja Baqi-Billa of Delhi giving this type of Tawajjuh to an inn-keeper. It is related that Khwaja Baqi-Billa happened to receive quite a number of guests, all unexpected, in the night. There being nothing to eat in the house, the saint was worried as to how to play the host towards them. A poor inn-keeper who was there at the time, observing the perplexity of the Master, offered to do the needful in the matter. The saint granted him permission. The inn-keeper went to his shop in the town and, returning with whatever eatables were available there, feasted the guests of the evening.

"At this the Master became extremely pleased with the inn-keeper and looking at him said, 'Demand anything you like at this moment. I promise to give it to you.' The poor inn-keeper, not knowing what to ask of the Master, simply said, 'Make me like unto your own self.' The saint was quite taken aback by this request, and tried to persuade him to ask for something else instead, in the form of untold wealth or even a kingdom. The inn-keeper replied, 'I have said my say and you have given your word.' Thereupon the saint had to give in and retired with the man into a private chamber. Inside the room the saint subjected the inn-keeper to his Ittehadi Tawajjuh and when, after half an hour, the Master and the disciple came out of the room, the people there failed to differentiate between the two. The Master and the disciple looked even physically alike. The only difference noticeable was that the inn-keeper was a little unsteady in his gait.

"Even in the animal kingdom something akin to Ittehadi Tawajjuh is practiced. There is an insect in the East called Anjanhari (a species of caterpillar) which never procreates in the ordinary way by laying eggs. When it is about to die, it brings another insect from the fields and concentrates upon it by droning away on the object of concentration for some length of time until the insect is transformed into its own likeness—that of a caterpillar. No sooner is this physical tranformation achieved than the original insect expires.

"4. The Qalabi Tawajjuh (spiritual concentration) is resorted to by Perfect Masters, and the disciples who are subjected to it become gradually perfect like the Master in the course of a few months, years or decades. The effect of this Tawajjuh, unlike the first two mentioned, is permanent, and once attained it can never be taken away or spoiled by anything morally wrong, such as drink, fornication, theft or a lie. It is this Tawajjuh I am imparting to my disciples.

"There is another type of Tawajjuh which I need mention here. It is called Ifaqiya Tawajjuh (restorative concentration). This Tawajjuh is given by a Master to a disciple after realization, when the latter refuses to return to normality from the enjoyment of the highest state of consciousness. When a disciple is required to return to the normal state of consciousness for the performance of the duty devolving upon him towards humanity, the Master uses this Tawajjuh to wean him away from the state of the highest divine bliss to the plane of painful duty on earth."

January 1939

Question: Can some idea be had of what sound is like from the higher planes? Does it in any way differ in intensity of frequency of vibration from the sound of the physical plane?

Answer: " This is rather difficult to explain and still more difficult to understand, as it relates to subjective experience. However, know this: that sound is present throughout all the seven planes, differing in its expression of feeling and bliss.

"The sound, sight or smell of the higher planes can by no stretch of the imagination be likened to what we are used to on the physical plane. It is something altogether different in nature, quality and expression; but all the same, for the sake of description and analogy, we can do no better than use the familiar terms, viz., sound, sight and smell. Our physical organs of hearing, seeing and smelling are useless for experiencing and enjoying the higher planes. Therein it is a different eye that sees, a different ear that hears, and a different nose that smells. You know already that there are inner senses, a counterpart of the external senses in man, and it is the former that experience the higher planes.

"Avoiding the mistake of describing the sound of the higher planes as something differing in intensity and frequency of vibrations from the sound of the physical plane, know for a certainty that there is actually what may be called 'sound' in the first three planes. The form, beauty, music and bliss of this sound is beyond description. The celestial music (sound) is peculiar to the first plane and can be experienced or induced by the mantric force. It is on account of this that even an unintelligent repetition or reading of scriptures is encouraged and advocated. As stated above, although there is sound in all the seven planes, it is smell that is peculiar to the second and third planes; and sight belongs to the fifth and sixth planes. In the fourth plane the bliss of sound, smell and sight are all subdued and repressed. The fourth plane connotes the darkest night of the spiritual journey, wherein even Jesus could not but cry out: 'My God, my God, why hast Thou forsaken me?'

"It is for this reason that the wayfarer traversing the path all alone, unaided by a Master and finding himself benighted and forlorn in the fourth plane, is very strongly tempted to make wrong use of his psychic powers of the three lower planes, culminating in the fourth as 'siddhis' (kashf-o-karmat). And what a fall this means! It means once again going through the chain of evolution right from the beginning—the stone state.

"The seventh plane stands unique. The sound, sight and smell here is divine in essence and has no comparison to that emanating from the lower planes. In this plane one does not hear, smell or see, but actually becomes sound, smell and sight simultaneously and is divinely conscious of it.

"The different religious practices and the yogas, after establishing contact with the higher planes, induce experiences peculiar to those planes. For instance, contacting the first plane (sound) engenders inspiration; the second and third planes (smell) beget intuition; the fifth and sixth (sight) give illumination. The experience of the fifth and sixth, the Sufis term as 'marefat' (gnosis). The seventh plane stands for revelation and this, according to Sufis, is haqiqat (reality)."

Question: Will material science, in the near or remote future, be able to probe into subtle and higher planes? At the present rate of scientific progress it ought to be possible, if there be continuity or a point of fusion from the material to the subtle.

Answer: "You are going into deeper waters. Now listen carefully. The soul, essentially divine, infinite in existence, knowledge and bliss is, all by itself, the only Reality. Everything else exists only in imagination. The famous and oft-repeated parable of the snake and rope will elucidate the point. The soul somehow imagined the rope to be the snake. This phase engendered fear which, to stretch the simile further, we may call mind. The mind extended itself to grasp it (the snake); this is energy, and actually grappling it means body. Thus we see mind, energy, body, although all three have no existence except in imagination; but in relation to each other they are altogether distinct, separate and independent.

"Although mind emanates energy and energy in essence is mind, nevertheless in expression and form both are distinct and apart. Similarly, body is the outcome of energy, and though identical in essence the function and formation is radically different and independent. To illustrate the point, let us take thread to be mind, and cloth made thereof to represent energy, and clothing to signify body. The cloth here is of thread, but in utility and form is altogether different from thread. The clothing, say a coat, is from thread, but in form and expression is obviously and distinctly apart from cloth and thread. The making of cloth and coat from thread is easy and possible, but the return of the coat and cloth to the state of the original thread means the destruction and annihilation of the form and expression of both. Similarly, the emanation of energy and matter from mind is automatic and natural; but the return of matter and energy to mind is almost impossible. This return business is the beginning of spirituality.

"You must have felt by now your question answered by realizing how impossible it is for science to probe the subtle and higher planes. Science is, as yet, a long way off; it has up to now only touched the fringe of the matter. It may, at the most, touch the extreme limits of matter but that will take ages. And who, till then, can vouch for the integrity of this—the present civilization?"

Question: For an aspirant to the Path in search
of a Master, is there any infallible method of
recognizing a Perfect Master?

Answer: "Spiritual attainment to the planes one
may not satisfactorily allocate or discriminate. All
those from the first to the sixth plane come under
the general category of 'advanced souls,' more or
less. But when luckily one comes into contact with
Perfection, there are unmistakable signs for a seeker
of truth who is patient and sincere.

"There are three important factors that are
characteristic of the state of Perfection. First,
Perfection is not only 'Oneness with God' but the
continued and uninterrupted experience of Oneness
in everything. A Perfect Master continuously,
without any break, experiences or realizes His own
Self as the Self in all. This inner experience
objectively manifests itself in the spontaneity of
Love that such a one feels or expresses towards all
creation. To Him nothing is attractive or repulsive:
good, bad; saint, sinner; beauty, ugliness; wisdom,
idiocy; health, disease are all different modes and
moods of His own manifestation. When embodied
Perfection loves, fondles, feeds any living creature, it
feels and enjoys as if it is loving, fondling and
feeding its own Self. In this state no vestige of
'otherness' is left.

"The second point is the undeniable atmosphere
of bliss that Perfection radiates in its immediate
vicinity and which a visitor cannot help feeling or
noticing. A Perfect Master not only enjoys infinite
bliss, but also experiences universal suffering. The
poignancy of suffering, however, is nullified and
subdued by the overwhelming joy or feeling of bliss.
Hence, Perfection outwardly always appears

blissfully calm and unperturbed in the face of every kind of pain, persecution and penury.

"The third most outstanding characteristic of Perfection is its power to adapt itself to any level or strata of humanity. It is as nonchalant on a throne as it is obviously indifferent and undisturbed in a gutter. It is impecunious with the poor, extravagant with the rich, lordly with kings, wise with the learned, and naively simple and innocent with the illiterate and ignorant. Just as a Master of Arts delivers or teaches English in a different way to a beginner than to an undergraduate, similarly, a Perfect Master adapts Himself to the level of the one whom He wants to uplift spiritually. Each one according to his need, and each one according to his aptitude, is the perennial plan of personified Perfection."

December 1938

Question: What is the spiritual significance of a mantra (Persian "Zikr")? How is a neophyte helped by a monotonous incantation or repetition of a certain word or words?

Answer: "A mantra is very beneficial to a neophyte on the spiritual path, particularly so when it is given by the guru. The first and immediate result accruing from frequent repetition of a word or words is the concentration of the mind on the subject to be gained. Secondly, the sound vibrations as a result of continuous repetition induce, in the course of time, harmonious sympathy to the sound vibrations of the higher planes, engendering a blissful feeling—a factor greatly encouraging to a beginner. This blissful feeling, coupled with the awakening of mental powers, is called the Mantric force, and it has immense possibilities for good as well as bad."

Question: The astronomical phenomena, the eclipse of the moon or the sun, visibly stir the Hindu world into great religious activity. Why is such an occurrence as an eclipse deemed opportune for a fresh flux of religious fervor, particularly in the matter of perfecting some mantras?

Answer: **"The eclipse is purely an astronomical phenomenon and needs no explanation. There is, however, a germ of spiritual truth behind the grotesquely colorful imagery of gods and demons, their squabbles and jealousies for the nectar of immortality, all ingeniously concocted by the priest-class to flabbergast the superstitious masses and incidentally to fleece them.**

"The spiritual aspect of the question is this: The whole universe, known and unknown, has come out of a point in the microcosm which may be called the Creation Point. Simultaneously with this emanation two processes come into play—evolution and production. The differences between the two processes are rather significant and must be clearly understood. The process of production is dependent on the process of evolution in sequence of causation, but not in the sequence of time. Evolution depends on the Creation Point for cause, but production is dependent on evolution. Evolution connotes spiritual progress and production signifies material growth and change, organic and inorganic.

"It is a scientifically acknowledged fact that the stellar regions, planets and stars, do exert an influence on the life and activity of this planet—the earth. And since this earth of ours has the highest evolved organic life, the human happens to be the nearest to the spiritual plane; the phenomenon of eclipse does indirectly affect the world spiritually.

"The Rishis of old knew all too well the astronomical basis and the spiritual influence of such a heavenly occurrence. Looking at the average mentality of the masses of their time, the Rishis could do no better than issue cut-and-dried instructions as to prayers, penance and austerities, investing the whole affair with a religious importance rather than give a rational and spiritual elucidation. In course of time the religious 'do's and don'ts' of the wise Rishis were very cleverly woven round by self-seeking priests, with a picturesque and awe-inspiring legend of the gods, demons, nectar, the moon in travail and its subsequent Moksha (freedom) for purposes all too patent to thinking minds. Such legendary superstitions persist and flourish with ignorance and illiteracy; but now people are outgrowing such childish beliefs. There is, however, no denying the fact that a few prayers and ordeals undergone with keen concentration, concurrently with the eclipse of the sun or moon, do result in great spiritual benefit to the individual concerned."

Questions Meher Baba Answers

(These questions were asked by Mr. Garrett
Fort [Hollywood, California], a Western
disciple of Meher Baba, when he
was in India in 1936.)

Question: If all the beautiful things we have
known—moonlight, stars, music, the sound of the
sea, the fragrance of flowers, our little dreams—are
Maya, what is there left to take their place when you
sweep them out of our hearts and minds and leave
only the concept of a very far-off and abstract goal—
Realization? For until we are realized, it leaves us
with nothing but emptiness—and very sad.

Answer: **"Beauty and ugliness have relative
existence. To one trudging along under a scorching
sun, barefooted, with an empty stomach, Maya
outside won't look beautiful. The mood of the
subject (the perceiver) invests the object (the
perceived) with its own coloring.**

**"The goal of Realization does not necessarily
imply, for an average man, denial of things good or
bad. It only emphasizes its relative worth. From the
heights of Realization, Maya would cease to exist; it
was pure imagination. Even apart from the spiritual
experience, the conception that you are in the world
but not of the world would go a long way in
dissipating sadness and the feeling of void—of
emptiness.**

"If one were to treat sincerely and whole-heartedly Maya as pure imagination, the resultant poise and non-identification with things external would automatically open up this internal fountain of bliss and, instead of feeling sad and empty, one would be able to live the perfect life of being in harmony with the universe."

Question: Shall we, who dare not entertain what, to us, is the presumptuous hope of attaining Realization at this point in our journey, finish this life with none of the small but beautiful things that we, as human beings, have been used to turn to for solace?

Answer: "It all depends on whether what you term as solace is elevating or degrading. Recourse to alcohol for drowning one's sorrows is the perverted form of solace. Solace afforded by things outside of you is synonymous with doping, which gives a certain amount of momentary relief or relaxation. Real and unalloyed solace is within you.

"It is never presumptuous for anyone to hope for Realization. It is the goal of creation and the birthright of humanity. Blessed are they who are prepared to assert that right in this very life."

Question: You have said that to keep this love for You of Your disciples unalloyed, You must humor the less noble aspects of their nature, such as pride, jealousy, etc. How great can their love be if they have to be spiritually bribed to keep it alive and uppermost? And by fostering the very things that should be destroyed, how can their progress be speeded up? Doesn't this hold it back, make it more difficult all around?

Answer: "Up to a stage, the love of disciples can never be said to be perfect. The Beloved up to a point is constrained to humor the lovers (disciples) for the purpose of drawing them nearer. This nearness to the Beloved in turn fans the fire of love, which no sooner achieves Perfection than it automatically destroys in the lovers (disciples) the less noble aspects and traits of their nature."

Question: What is meant by the phrase "turning the key" which you so often utter? And what effect does it have on the lives of those to whom it is applied?

Answer: "Masters, as a rule, work and bring about results of a spiritual or material character in a natural way. On rare and important occasions, however, they have to disregard the natural law and bring about the desired result by psychic powers. A physician, for instance, does his best to feed a patient by way of mouth—a natural method. But when a patient is unable or refuses to take nutrition in the regular manner, the physician, bent upon restoring his health, resorts to rectal feeding. This is what I mean by 'turning the key.' "

April 1941

Question: Are there seven rays, as told about in occult books, and are there Masters who function on those respective rays?

Answer: "The seven rays with their peculiar characteristics are a symbolic expression of the seven stages of the return journey of a realized soul to normal consciousness. Those realized beings who have a duty to perform on the material plane have to come down to normal consciousness and take their stand at one of the seven stages of the return journey best suited for the fulfillment of their task. These seven stages of their return journey have their peculiar features and characteristics, and these are reflected in the outward circumstances and living conditions of a Master. For instance, one Master lives on earth like a prince, another lives a life of poverty and austerity. One is in the midst of the busy world, and another in strict seclusion. The powers (Siddhis, Tajalliyat) are peculiar to different stages and their expression determines the particular plane from which a Master is working."

Question: Where is the "Hall of Learning" of which I have read and where those on earth are taken as they progress to take the first few initiations? Books allegedly written by Hilarion describe it impressively, telling of the great hosts of souls who stand within it, veiled, thinking themselves alone until their veils are raised with various initiations. Here take place the ceremonies of the soul that begin in December and last until Easter. Is all this true, or is it just told as symbolism?

Answer: " 'Hall of Learning' is pure symbolism. It is analogous to the Sufistic belief and picture of 'Darbare-e-Mohammedi,' i.e., the court of Mohammed. The inner court presided over by Mohammed in person, and the outer court presided over by deputies, and the outermost court consisting of those prepared souls clamoring for entry, is almost similar to the picture drawn by Hilarion, as you say."

Question: Is it impertinent to ask why You are focussing our attention on such a high goal, rather than showing us the lower planes and giving us understanding of their properties and functions? The high ideal is so remote from our understanding that it leaves us empty, unsatisfied, still as blind as ever, like a class of children listening to the nebular theory.

Answer: "There is no higher or lower goal. There is only one goal, i.e., self-realization. The journey of the planes, from one to another, is like changing one prison cell for another, or amounts to exchanging iron fetters for golden ones. In neither case is one free; and it is perfect freedom from the bindings of the physical and the spiritual planes that I aim for. The advancements on the planes may connote progress and be attitude-tempting to the wayfarer, but the allurements of a plane, once entered, are difficult to shake off. In fact the bindings (sanskaras) of the physical plane are much more easy to destroy than the bindings of the astral planes. I wish you to be free once and forever.

"The lower planes are the result of imagination and are based on illusion; however, I shall some day explain the lower planes in a manner practical and understandable even to a layman."

Question: Do You want us to accept everything that You tell us, blindly, whether we understand it or not, or may we ask questions?

Answer: **"No, I do not want you to accept everything blindly. I like discrimination and a sense of humor. You may ask questions, but the most necessary ones."**

Question: Is there really the place known as "Shamballa," the astral center where the Masters dwell in disembodied form?

Answer: **"You know already that planes are not places. The state and stage connoting 'Shamballa' exists. There is difference of terminology only. This is known as 'Vidnyan' in Sanskrit."**

Question: What are the psychic, mental or spiritual reactions to preserving silence, as You do for so long, and in what degree are our organizations affected by the same practice over a short period of time?

Answer: **"Universal mind and infinite consciousness have infinite ways of working universally. So whatever work one of infinite mind and universal consciousness does, it reverberates throughout the universe and produces reflex action.**

If He fasts, the result of the fasting is felt by the whole universe spiritually. A Master's working is always for the spiritual end. If He observes silence, the same result is brought about.

"Now the whole world is laboring under terrible economic chaos. To follow the spiritual path and to enable the mind to accept the spiritual, the material needs to an extent must be satisfied. So when I with My own hands give food and clothing to the poor, the result will be that the world will gain in economic and material welfare. When I give the mad and the lepers a wash, the result will be that those of subnormal and abnormal consciousness, and lepers, will either get cured or their future births will be greatly minimized.

"When I ask any one of you to bathe a leper, your doing it serves a dual purpose. In the first place, you are trained to tackle difficult and disagreeable work, which ultimately from the spiritual standpoint results in the gradual elimination of the ego; and secondly, the habit of obeying My orders implicitly and unquestionably is developed. For example, if I ask you to observe silence and if you have had sufficient grounding in the matter of obeying Me unquestionably, no other extraneous consideration will deter you from undertaking the task.

"Also, as you are near to Me and connected with Me, your observance of fast or silence or bathing of the leper, etc., will affect the whole range of your work with Me."

Questions Meher Baba Answers

by Dr. C. D. Deshmukh, Lecturer
Morris College, Nagpur

Question: If after the best use of the intellect a man comes to the conclusion that God does not exist, should he not stick to his conclusion?

Answer: **"As long as the conclusion does not lead you to moral evil, it does not matter. Such conclusion is an instance of the veiling of the truth by the operation of the intellect. When the time is ripe, the truth is gradually unveiled."**

Question: Sometimes a person feels like asking many questions of the Master. What does this indicate about his spiritual preparation?

Answer: **"There are three stages of the disciple. In the first stage the Master draws the disciple to Himself. This is the stone stage. The disciple is enwrapped in deep ignorance and has no sense of spiritual values. He cannot know the Master at this stone stage and the initiative is entirely with the Master.**

"The second stage is called the worm stage. Just as the worm is engaged in all kinds of movements and actions, so the mind of the disciple is active in all kinds of doubts and questions. At this stage the disciple asks many questions of the Master. There is constant movement of thought at this worm stage.

"The third stage is called the dog stage. At this stage the mind has no questions to ask. It is in a

faith-state. Just as the dog follows the Master without challenge or doubt, the disciple has unswerving faith in the Master, and follows His instructions unfailingly. At this stage asking comes to an end. When spiritual progress has not yet begun, as well as when it is at its height, there is no asking of the Master."

Meher Baba with two favorite pets, Kippy and Canute.

Meher Baba
An Interview

by Dr. P. S. Ramnathan, Prof. of Philosophy,
King Edward College

Last December, in response to the kind invitation of
a friend who is also a great admirer and devotee of
Meher Baba, I went to Nagpur to have the darshan
and the first-hand experience of the Master. Meher
Baba impressed me with His intellectual depth and
clarity. In the second interview I asked Him what I
regard as the question of questions concerning man's
life and destiny. I requested Him to enlighten me on
the problem of salvation by expounding on the true
relation of the individual to the whole.

Question: Has the individual any destiny apart
from the whole of which he is a part? Is it right for
the individual to seek private salvation? His
fulfillment consists in losing himself in the whole and
living for it; and it seems that he can never be
anything more than a part of the whole.

Answer: **"When we think of the individual we at
once grasp it as something limited, so it cannot be
identical with the unlimited whole. You are right in
saying that the individual must lose himself in the
whole, but the matter does not rest there. We may
compare the individual to the drop, and the whole to
the ocean. The drop is separate from the ocean and
again merges into it. What then is the purpose of its
being separated if it is merely to merge itself again**

in the way in which it was originally merged? Evolution would be fruitless if we end where we started. The individual has to retain his individuality and realize his unity with the whole consciously. Thus Christ realizes God as Christ. You realize God as yourself. It is a personal realization."

Question: Is there any technique of realizing the goal apart from the total process of life itself? Are we right in giving more importance to knowledge (dnyana) than to action (karma)?

Answer: "All paths are really one. Karma Yoga when rightly interpreted is right. There is no dnyana without karma and there is no karma without dnyana."

The extraordinary charm of His personality; the joy and love radiating from His face, transfiguring all those who came before Him; His intellectual acumen and the utter absence of self-consciousness—all these have tended to make me cherish my visit to Him as a treasured memory.

SAYINGS
OF MEHER BABA

There is nothing but God.

Only three things are of real worth: God, Love and the Perfect Master. These three are almost one and the same.

It is the same one Paramatman or Supreme Soul who is playing the different parts of the Almighty, the Creator (Ishwar), Shivatman, and Jivatman.

The Almighty, the Supreme Soul, God, is beyond even the super-conscious state. He is infinite; He is the shoreless ocean of Truth. As Ishwar He is the creator, preserver, and destroyer of the universe.

The individual or ordinary consciousness that has not realized God is finite and limited.

The Shivatman or God-realized man knows Himself as the Almighty, the one infinite ocean of Truth. He has attained the Christ-conscious state. Shivatman is the Sadguru or Perfect Master. He knows that He is in every man (Jivatman) and that every Jivatman is in Him. The Perfect Master is Love, Lover and the Beloved.

In order to realize God and to gain the original state from which everything emerged, we should follow the creed that accords with our own conscience and stick to that path which best suits our spiritual tendency, our mental attitude, our physical aptitude, and our external surroundings and circumstances.

God-realization is not to be confused with intellectual conviction regarding God and creation; just as the head is not to be confused with the hair nor the thing itself with its shadow.

Beware of pride, not only because it is hydra-headed, but because it is deceptive. So deceptive is it that, more often than not, it puts on the apparel of humility.

A lustful man, no matter what good qualities he may possess, cannot move along the spiritual path; he is like a cart with one wheel.

When a person is in Yoga Samadhi his mind is temporarily dead, but his intellect and egoism are there just the same; and no sooner does the state of Samadhi pass than his egoism begins to work. Nirvikalpa Samadhi is higher than and quite different from Yoga Samadhi. Before a person can expect to enjoy Nirvikalpa Samadhi his intellect and egoism must disappear in order to make room for Dnyan or real spiritual knowledge.

Although the gross sphere is the outcome of the subtle sphere and is dependent upon it, the subtle sphere is completely independent of the gross or physical world.

The Jivatman, the individual or unrealized soul, is in the bindings of the mind, the subtle and the gross bodies. Its bindings are both of the mind and of the body. But when the Jivatman crosses these bindings and becomes Shivatman, the realized soul, one with God, there are no desires left.

Profound worship based on high ideals of philosophy and spirituality, and prompted by Divine Love, constitutes true mysticism (Bhakti Yoga). It follows then that the various ceremonies and rituals which are part and parcel of every creed (the shariat of every religion) constitute only its shadow.

High spiritual truth has nothing to do with creeds, religions or shariat. It is far beyond the limited dogmas and doctrines of every creed. You will attain to this truth if you give up worldly Maya—lust, anger and greed.

Just as a random thought can manifest force in the shape of a bodily action, so meditation or deep and properly organized thinking produces a force of its own which is very useful to the spiritual aspirant. The manifestation of this force may not become evident immediately, or in a short time, but meditation is sure eventually to bear fruit.

It is unnecessary to lay down hard and fast rules regarding the posture in meditation. The sitting posture, or kneeling, whichever you find most convenient, should be adopted. But once it is adopted you must stick to it and sit in the same way daily.

There is no length of time which can be called too long for meditation, and every hour of the night and the day is suitable; but the best period for meditation is the early hours of the morning: four to seven a.m.

For those who insist from the very depths of their souls and from the innermost cores of their hearts on seeing Reality face to face, at all costs and consequences, there is only one way—that of complete renunciation.

Take good care of your body, but do not be a slave to it. If you think constantly of its welfare, you are like the miser who thinks constantly of his gold.

In the ordinary sense of the word it is correct to call very fine substances—such as ether, atoms, vibrations, light and space—subtle. They are unquestionably matter, though in a very fine form. In talking of spiritual concerns, subtle means something completely contrary to material or physical, however fine or attenuated these gross things may be.

The difference between antar drashti (spiritual insight) and atman-drashti (spiritual sight) is great indeed. The former means seeing the subtle universe, but spiritual sight means seeing God and seeing Him everywhere.

    With the gross eye gross things are seen; with the subtle or internal eye the subtle world and the planes are seen; and with the spiritual eye God is seen.

To attain to the state of the highest, three different routes have to be chalked out. They are Bhakti, Dnyan and Karma (devotion, spiritual knowledge and service). The aspirant has to pass through three principal stages: they are the gross, or physical, the subtle or astral, and the mind spheres.

Miracles performed by yogis are essentially selfish, as they are invariably based on personal, egoistic motives; whereas the miracles of Sadgurus, or Perfect Masters, are absolutely selfless, as they are based on the principle of giving a spiritual push to humanity.

It is the mind that makes us slaves to worldly desires. The mind also can enable us to become the masters of destiny and to realize the supreme Self.

Just as the unreality of a dream is only appreciated on awakening from sleep, so to experience the gross creation with all its apparent realities and tangibilities as a mere vacant dream, one has to be fully conscious of the subtle and mind spheres.

The body is but the outer covering of your soul. It is Maya that makes you identify yourself with the body and which makes you forgetful of your eternal, indivisible, resplendent divinity.

Nature never has been, never will be, and never is at war with man. It seems as if she is at war with man because he violates her laws. No individual and no nation can break her laws with impunity.

To see God means to cease seeing everything except God. What does it mean to be supra-conscious? It means to be fully conscious of unconsciousness; that is, to be conscious of nothing but the divine Self.

To be virtuous out of vanity is little better than to be vicious out of perversity.

Miracles, whether performed by Perfect Masters or by yogis, are mere illusions in comparison with the everlasting truth, and are not more real than the shadows of this world.

Spirit communication is the experience of the semi-subtle by the physical senses in the conscious state. It is not a sign of advancement on the Divine Path and has nothing to do with its goal (gnosis).

He is indeed a brave man who in time of adversity feels the happiness of prosperity and who, though oppressed on all sides, remains calm and balanced.

What food is to the body, the body, to some extent, is to the soul. When food is thrown off in the form of refuse, you do not lament; neither should you mourn when the body is given up at death.

Section Four

Discourses, Messages
and Explanations
by Meher Baba

I Am The Infinite One
Meher Baba
Extract from Meher Baba's letter to H. Von F.

"The East already knows Me; I have some thousands of followers in India and Persia.

"I have not chosen the West; it is not a question of choice, but a question of where My work is most needed to have spirituality and materialism go hand in hand.

"There are hundreds of religious teachers in the East who call themselves pundits, well versed in scriptures and full of wise sayings to fit any eventuality; but there are very few who have achieved personal experience of the highest One. The real thing is to feel, to experience and to realize the One Infinite Consciousness; and that is possible only through love and is inspired by contact with a Perfect Master; without that contact none has attained Perfection.

"The true life is lived when one feels heart and head balanced, intellect and feeling linked, materialism and spirituality blended. Then only can one realize the infinite in every phase of life and be in harmony with everyone and everything, living in the world of matter yet feeling detached; so being identified with the One Personal God.

"There are two aspects of the Infinite One— personal and impersonal. The impersonal lies beyond the domain of creation and transcends even the mental plane. The personal aspect of God is the

Meher Baba at the mast ashram in Bangalore, 1939.

Perfect Master who, having attained to the impersonal aspect, lives in the world and, using Maya, helps others towards Truth.

"I never wish to be called Redeemer, Savior, Divine Majesty and so on. The disciples through their love, faith, enthusiasm gave such titles. There are many who misunderstand Me, call Me Satan, anti-Christ; but to Me it is all the same. I know what I am.

"I see My own life in everyone, and so continually realize that I am the Infinite One; and this 'I' is not the outcome of the limited finite egoism, but it is the outcome of actual experience of the highest state.

"When an Avatar has to manifest, for some period before His manifestation He either fasts, keeps silent, or adopts some inner discipline for the benefit of the world. He does not do this for His own sake because, having attained to the Highest, nothing is left for Him to do for His own self. But before manifestation, whatsoever He does, His mind is universal.

"Buddha never ate food cooked by others.

"Jesus fasted forty days.

"I keep silent."

Meher Baba's Message to His Disciples

(Given on His return from Calcutta)
Meherabad, Ahmednagar, June 21, 1940

The present world crisis, chaos and universal
suffering are absolutely necessary for the eventual
spiritual upliftment and for a new world wherein
peace, love and Divine aspirations will reign
supreme. None should therefore feel scared and
dismayed, bearing in mind the certainty of this
bright future.

"From the spiritual point of reality, the words
national and foreign, killed and killer, war and peace,
success and defeat, have no existence and are
imaginary dreams; and the present universal chaos is
just a universal nightmare necessary for the
universal awakening.

"Body-forms and minds are innumerable and of
infinite variety, but souls are all originally and
eternally One. In fact, only One infinite reality
exists and that is God. So this apparent world
catastrophe is, by Divine will, essential for a Divine
manifestation in the near future of love and real
peace, in which I have to play the greatest part.

"Men and women all over the world who care to
share in My work can do so by trying their utmost
to maintain a pure character; and to avoid strictly
feelings of lust and enmity in any form. To try not
to be the victims of fears nor of the weaknesses of
lying and back-biting; in personal quarrels never to

attack anyone save in defending the weak, but to do even that absolutely without hatred; to meditate on Divine Love for any period every day, according to individual circumstances; and to observe fast (either to remain on milk and water, or on water and one meal during 24 hours) once a week, for a period of twelve months, from the 1st of August 1940 to 31st of July 1941.

"I shall remain in seclusion during this period of one year and no correspondence will be attended to, except telegraphic communications in most urgent and serious matters."

Meher Baba's Message on the Spiritual Significance of the Present War

"Two kinds of forces are operative in the present war: (1) the forces which make for love, justice, harmony and the well-being of mankind taken as a whole and (2) the forces which in alliance with narrow racial or national loyalties work towards the selfish exploitation of others. This war is bringing a vast amount of suffering and destruction to millions of people. But all this will not be in vain. Out of this chaos there will emerge a new world of freedom and happiness and understanding.

"War can at best be only a means to an end; it can never be an end in itself. It is therefore imperatively necessary for the war lords to search their own hearts and to make sure that the ends for which they are fighting are a reflection of the Divine plan which is to lead humanity to a spiritual brotherhood, cemented by an inviolable sense of the unity of all human beings, irrespective of the distinctions based on class, color, nationality, race, religion or creed. War effort will be justified or stand condemned not by the results which it produces, but by the ends by which it is inspired. The world has to face this war and go through its ordeal of fire, even at the cost of irreparable damage and unredeemable suffering; it is a necessary evil.

"Even in itself war is not an unmixed evil since it calls forth and releases, under the stress of imminent danger, much action which disregards the limited self and is inspired by the impersonal spirit of welcoming sacrifice and suffering for the safety and prosperity of fellow-beings. It is better that such unselfish action be released under the stimulus of danger than that it should not be released at all. It is better that men should forget their petty selves under the pressure of a collective calamity than that they should be permanently encased in the ignoble pursuit of personal safety and in the ruthless attempt to perpetuate separative existence and interests. War effort generates and fosters many qualities of spiritual importance; it is therefore not altogether without spiritual significance, even when it is considered in itself. And when war effort is forced upon a nation or a people for the sake of higher values and impersonal considerations of well-being, it becomes not only spiritually defensible but inevitable.

"People ought to face the incidents of war with courage and equanimity, in the faith that no sacrifice or suffering is too much when the call of duty is clear and imperative. In the event of a direct and aggressive attack the clear duty of all is to resist it, even by direct participation in war, if there is no other alternative. But in offering such resistance they shall make sure that they are prompted solely by the sense of duty and that they have no hatred or bitterness towards the aggressor, who is acting under spiritual ignorance. Further, they shall not be callous to the physical or mental suffering inflicted by air-raids or by warfare on land or sea. On the contrary, they shall render to the wounded and desolate victims of war every possible service, according to their individual ability and aptitude.

"As a rule spiritual aspirants are indifferent to purely material well-being. They are prone to be indifferent to war as well as war-effort on the grounds that most wars are actuated by purely material considerations. But it is a mistake to divorce spiritual from material considerations; material considerations do have a spiritual aspect and importance. Even spiritual aspirants, who are wrapped up in the super-sensible realities of inner life, can ill afford to ignore war, particularly when they are directly involved in it. Spiritual aspirants take their stand upon the reality and the eternity of the infinite soul; it should therefore be easy for them to stake everything for the sake of a duty which springs from the claims of the spirit.

"When truly understood, all conflicts and wars are seen to be a part of the Divine game; they are thus a result of the Divine will which finds expression in the world of manifestation, through the help of Maya or the cosmic power which creates and sustains the illusory world of duality. The purpose served by Maya in the Divine game is twofold: (1) it can be instrumental in entrapping the soul in the mazes of illusion and (2) it can also be instrumental in freeing the soul from the clutches of spiritual ignorance and bondage. Maya should not be ignored; it must be handled with detachment and understanding. Wars are the working of Maya; they are spiritually disastrous or otherwise, according to whether they are inspired by attachment or detachment from the creations of Maya.

"From the spiritual point of view of the last and only truth, all souls are, in their essence, fundamentally one. War cannot create any real cleavage or division between the people who are fighting with each other. The people of the warring countries seem to be different from each other merely by virtue of having different bodies and minds; but from the point of view of their souls, all differences are not only secondary but false. The spiritual unity of all souls remains inviolable in spite of all wars; and from the point of view of ultimate reality it remains true that no soul is really at war with any other soul. There is a war in different ideologies; and this war of ideologies extends to and involves not only the minds but also the bodies of the people; but the undivided and indivisible soul remains one in its unimpeachable and integral unity.

"The spiritually advanced persons are alive to this truth of the unity of all souls; and the role which they play in the game of God is necessarily determined by the spiritual understanding which they have. They perform their duty in cooperation with the Divine will; and, being in tune with the infinite truth, they are, in playing their part, not only free from all thoughts of selfish gain, but also from the reactionary feelings of hate or malice or revenge.

"The soul remains untouched and unscathed by the loss and the destruction of material things and possessions; and death is only a gateway to further life. Those who would play their part in the Divine game shall remain unmoved by any bereavements or losses; and they shall also impart to others the spirit of cheerful resignation to the Divine will. The un-understood sufferings of war will embitter many souls; they need to be helped in the restoration of unassailable faith and imperishable sweetness of life. Those who are initiated into the eternal values of inner life shall bear the burden of dispelling unwarranted gloom and depression and cheering up those who are in anguish.

"In the hour of trial let the thought of everyone

be not for the limited self, but for others—not for the claims of the ego-life, but for the claims of the Divine Self which is equally in all. It is a mistake to ignore human suffering as merely a part of the illusory universe. Not by ignoring human suffering, but by handling it with creative love, is the gateway opened for life eternal; and not through callous indifference, but through active and selfless service, is secured the attainment of that transcendental and illimitable truth which is at the heart of the illusory universe.

"The last but not the least duty of those who would stand by reason and love is to see war, as well as war-effort, in the right perspective, as being only the means for the goal of peace and understanding. It is not possible to justify war apart from the end which is sought through it. War does not stand justified merely by the spiritual qualities which it generates and fosters; these qualities can also be developed in times of peace. It is time that humanity is imbued with the spontaneous spirit of love and service, needing no stimulus of danger for the release of impersonal and unselfish action.

"Though it seems difficult, humanity has to emerge out of this dreadful war with unimpaired spiritual integrity; with hearts free from the poison of malice or revenge; with minds disburdened of the blows given or received; with souls unscathed by suffering and filled with the spirit of unconditional surrenderance to the Divine will which shall ensoul and inspire post-war humanity. In spite of its attendant evils, this war shall play its part in My mission of helping humanity to fulfill the Divine plan on earth and to inherit the coming era of truth and love, of peace and universal brotherhood, of spiritual understanding and unbounded creativity.

"Apropos of numerous inquiries from My

followers, seeking guidance and instructions in the eventuality of the war directly and palpably affecting India, I have to call upon all concerned to go about their routine avocations, duties and responsibilities in a spirit of detachment, love, charity and hope, and to observe the following instructions meant for the category in which they are placed:

To the Disciples

"1. They should be above party politics and should bear malice and ill-will towards none.

"2.They should observe all the precautionary measures of war for the civil population enforced by the government of the day.

"3. They should continue as usual discharging their special duties and work for My spiritual cause unless otherwise directed by Me.

"4. They should stick to their posts and appointments anywhere in India, under any trying circumstances, unless ordered by the government to evacuate under emergency regulations.

"5. They may undertake humanitarian and relief work of a non-sectarian character without identifying themselves with any party or political organization working in that direction, and strictly within the scope of time and leisure left over after the performance of spiritual duties enjoined by Me.

"6. They should extend spiritual solace and comfort to the people within the area of their contact and influence, with a view to counteracting the panicky state of their minds.

"7. Exceptional cases and circumstances requiring readjustment of routine lives may be communicated to Me.

"1. They may join the A.R.P. and home guard organizations of the government and any such humanitarian activities undertaken by non-official bodies like the Red Cross Ambulance Society and the League of Mercy.

"2. They may arrange their family affairs and business problems consistent with the urgency of the situation and in complete accord with the ordinances of the local government.

"3.They should undertake humanitarian and relief work independently or conjointly with any sectarian or political organization of their choice.

"In short, all should face the impending crisis, however painful and cruel it may turn out to be, with patience, fortitude and self-sacrifice, never for a moment forgetting the fact that the redemption of distracted humanity through Divine Love is very much nearer at hand than many care to believe."

Excerpt from
"Notes from My Diary"
by F. H. Dadachanji

Everyone knows how and what important decisions were being made at Delhi during the last week of March and the beginning of April. At such a crucial moment in the history of India, Meher Baba decided for His own reasons that his last message on the "Spiritual Significance of the Present War," as well as His article on "Violence and Non-violence," be read by all the important leaders of India who participated in these vital discussions.

Two of His disciples were deputed for this important work and were instructed to proceed to Delhi forthwith to personally deliver the message and the article to all the leaders. These instructions were duly carried out, and thirty of India's great leaders and most prominent people received Baba's message at a most opportune period.

When the two disciples returned to Dehra Dun and reported to Baba their interesting experiences, Baba remarked that His plan had been duly chalked out and was to be duly gone through at this significant time. Addressing the two disciples, Baba pointed out:

"I have contacted the leaders through you. The leaders will now take decisions according to the thoughts and wisdom God will give them. God's plan is always for the best and although at times

things appear to be going wrong, in fact it is not so.

"Real non-violence, like truth, love and selfless service, is the guide to God-realization. My non-violence includes violence, under certain circumstances, when it is done a hundred percent for others and without the slightest feeling of malice, hatred, revenge or self-gain; and I call it 'non-violent' violence."

MEHER BABA JOURNAL
June 1942

Excerpt from "Notes from My Diary"
In the Abode of Saints in the Himalayas
by F.H. Dadachanji

Violence and Non-violence

During the course of discussion on the subject of violence and non-violence, Meher Baba explained a few more things as follows:

"Non-violence, pure and simple, is the beyond state of God. It is the goal of humanity; it can't exist where one is still in the stages of a 'seeker,' but one can however reach this goal through the means of 'non-violence of the brave' or of 'selfless violence,' which means 'non-violent violence.'

"Beloved is the goal. Love is the means. The lover can reach the Beloved through love.

"God in the beyond state of Paramatman is love, light and life infinite. He is everything.

"Unless one realizes God and has love infinite, one cannot be purely and infinitely non-violent.

"God does not include violence; so does Love not include lust.

"Non-violence, pure and simple, is love infinite.

"A lover who is longing to see the Beloved is in the same stage and category as a 'seeker' on the path.

"A Majzub who has been one with the Beloved through love is in the same state as God.

"The difference between these stages may be explained in the following manner: suppose you are slapped or kicked by someone. If you do not retaliate but keep quiet and do nothing, it is in the category of a 'seeker' who practices 'non-violence of the brave.'

"In a similar case of a Majzub being slapped or kicked by someone, it is quite different. He has neither the necessity to keep quiet or control himself, nor has he to make an effort for same. For in his state of the Majzub, which is Divine intoxication, he doesn't at all 'feel' the slap or the kick. He has gone beyond that state of 'feeling.' The question of 'feeling' even after God-realization comes only when the God-realized being again comes down to the world of phenomena with normal consciousness. There he can use non-violence, pure and simple, which is based on Divine Love, and try to persuade the aggressor (the one who slapped or kicked) through infinite love. Because, in his beyond state, where all souls are one, he is himself both the 'striker and the 'stricken,' the 'aggressor' and the 'aggrieved.'

"It is either unity (oneness) or duality. There is no stage in-between.

"Different yogas have different means; e.g., for Bhakti Yoga, love; for Karma Yoga, non-violence, and so on.

"In Karma Yoga, love for individuals is non-violence of the brave.

"In Karma Yoga, love for the masses is non-violent violence.

"Beloved, in Karma Yoga, is non-violence, pure and simple. Now to reach the Beloved aspect, you have to go through the path of love.

"Why is God called 'Beloved'? Because we reach Him through love.

"When you reach Him through non-violence, you call Him infinite non-violence. Dnyani (the Wise Ones) call Him 'Infinite Chaitanya' (infinite consciousness). Those who follow Raja Yoga call him Prabhu (the maker and creator of everything). Thus God is named after the path through which one attains and realizes Him."

The Need For Creative Leadership in India

Discourse by Meher Baba

"Throughout the hoary ages of the past, India has played the most prominent part in shaping the spiritual history of humanity. She has been a home of Avatars, Prophets, Masters, seers and sages, whose contribution to the spiritual evolution of humanity has been unparalleled. The contribution of India to the solution of mundane problems has also been remarkable, since she has produced scientists, poets, philosophers, emperors, leaders and statesmen of the first order. In the past, India has attained eminence in spiritual as well as mundane spheres of life; and her place in the post-war New World of the Future is going to be unique.

"The problems which India has to face today are, in some ways, more complicated than the problems which any other country is called upon to solve. Men of all races, creeds, cults and religions have found a home in India; and if this lack of uniformity in composition has presented some difficulties in arriving at solidarity and concerted action in the national life of India, it must in no way be looked upon as a pure handicap. The various streams of culture which have poured into the life-history of India have added to the wealth of her national personality; and they have not only created a suitable opportunity for arriving at a new cultural synthesis, but have necessitated its emergence. If handled with creative leadership, the presence of conflicting elements in Indian life can be utilized for bringing into existence a rich world-culture, which shall not only rejuvenate and harmonize Indian life, but will also give a new tone to the life of the whole world.

"The process by which we arrive at the new world-culture cannot be purely mechanical. We can never have any vigorous world-culture by merely piling together certain isolated elements selected from the present diversity of culture; that way we shall only succeed in getting a patchwork of little vitality. A hodgepodge of collected ideas can never be a substitute for a direct and fresh perception of the Goal. The new world-culture will have to emerge from an integral vision of the Truth independently of existing traditions and not from the laborious process of selection and compilation of conserved values.

"The new world-culture which will emerge from integral vision will, however, automatically bring about cultural synthesis. Since the vision that inspires the new world-culture will be comprehensive, it will not negate the values of diverse traditions; nor will it have merely patronizing tolerance for them. On the contrary, it will express itself through active appreciation of the essentials of diverse religions and cultures. The vast vision of the Truth cannot be limited by any creed, dogma or sect; however, it helps men to transcend these limitations, not by blind and total denial of any value to the existing creeds, dogmas and sects, but by discovering, accentuating, unfolding and developing such facets of the Truth as might have been hidden in them.

"Evolving a transcendent and synthetic culture which will express the Infinite Truth is one task before India. The other task, for which India is particularly qualified, is to help other nations in arriving at mutual understanding and harmony. This second task, again, requires creative leadership which will have an unclouded perception of the mission which India has to fulfill in relation to the destinies of the other nations of the world. In her foreign policy India must in no way be a party to color prejudice and color war. Black, yellow and white are differences of the skin; they are not differences within the soul itself. Through her past history, India has been a link between the East and the West; and the two have come closer to each other through her.

"The third task before the creative leadership in India is to strive for political poise in spite of the difficult situation in which she is placed. India can never make her full contribution to the world unless she is free from political domination and fear of foreign aggression or conquest. If she is to fulfill her mission in the sisterhood of nations, India must be free to shape her own national life and to determine her policy towards other nations. But insistence upon this fundamental need should not be allowed to disturb her political poise. While leadership in India would be justified in striving for national freedom and self-determination, it must not allow itself to be vitiated by reactionary isolationism. In the same way, while discharging the clear duty of resisting foreign aggression, India should try to keep free from hate, malice or revenge.

"Aggression must be met with resistance; and here it is unpractical to insist upon non-violence. Pure non-violence or incorruptible love can come spontaneously only where duality has been completely transcended in the realization of the last and the only Truth; and non-violence of the brave is possible only for advanced souls who have, through rigorous discipline, eradicated from their mind all forms of greed and hate. But so far as the masses are concerned, it is undesirable to ask them to stick to the external formula of non-violence when it is their clear duty to resist aggression in self-defense or in the defense of other weak brothers. In the case of the unevolved masses, universal insistence upon non-violence can only lead to their being cowardly, irresponsible and inert. True love is no game of the faint-hearted and the weak; it is born of strength and understanding. The ideal of non-violence, in the face of aggression, is impracticable for the masses; and it will have a tendency to be readily used as a subterfuge for servile acceptance of ignoble conditions and contemptible desertion of a clear duty. In its enthusiasm for the highest ideal, wise leadership can in no way afford to lose all sense of the relative and the practical. Human evolution proceeds by gradual stages from selfish violence to unselfish violence, and then from non-violence of the brave to the pure and incorruptible non-violence of Truth as Infinite Love.

"All narrowness limits love. In India, as well as in every other part of the world, humanity is breaking itself into narrow groups based upon the superficial and ultimately false differences of caste, creed, race, nationality, religion or culture. Since these groups have been long accustomed to separative distrust and fear, they have indifference, contempt or hostility towards each other. All this is due to ignorance, prejudice and selfishness; and it can only be mended by fostering the spirit of mutuality which breaks through artificial isolationism, and which derives its strength from the sense of the inviolable unity of life as a whole. Creative leadership (which has so much scope in the soil of India) will have to recognize and emphasize the fact that all men are already united with one another not only by their co-partnership in the Great Divine Plan for Earth, but also by virtue of their all being equally the expression of One Life. No line of action can be really helpful or fruitful unless it is in entire harmony with this deep Truth. The future of humanity is in the hands of those who have vision."

MEHER BABA JOURNAL
November 1939

Meher Baba's Discourse on Suffering

In response to the question by one of the group: "Why do we suffer?" Meher Baba replied: **"Why should we be born? To take birth means to suffer.**

"When suffering leads to real eternal happiness we should not attach importance to this suffering. It is to eliminate suffering that suffering has to come. This suffering is unnecessary and self-inflicted; ninety-nine per cent of the world's suffering is self-inflicted and then people ask, 'Why must we suffer?' Great suffering means great liberation.

"What is ignorance if not suffering? War is no special suffering; do not people suffer all the time? It is the suffering due to ignorance that has to become less by war—which is one collective mass suffering. It is universal suffering which leads to war. People suffer because they are not satisfied; they want more and more. Ignorance gives rise to greed and vanity. If you want nothing, would you then suffer? But you do want. If you did not want anything, you would not suffer even in the jaws of a lion. Even without war everyone suffers physically.

"Mental suffering is worse than physical suffering. What the people of the world with limited vision think of suffering is only physical. They draw pictures of a bomb-stricken person, nose off, leg off, etc. Sometimes physical suffering tends to ease mental suffering. The world's idea of suffering and

of happiness is entirely limited. Happiness you have no idea of—that real happiness—is worth all the mental and physical suffering of the universe. Then all suffering becomes as if it were not. It was due to ignorance. Ignorance makes you jump at the sight of a cockroach—real happiness does not make you feel the teeth of a tiger in your body.

"Even those who are not God-realized and have no knowledge, they, too, can control their minds to such an extent that nothing makes them feel pain and suffering—even when being buried. One yogi, who had not even the smell of knowledge, through yoga had himself thrown into a tub of boiling oil and not only did he not feel the pain but he was not even burnt a little. This is not the spirit's control over matter; it is even lower—it is breath control. When I talk of knowledge, it is not ordinary knowledge, it is experience of Godhood. Knowledge of God means becoming God—then all else is zero. When the Master comes down from Godhood to normal, the Master brings down God. He is not aloof from God for one second but He has to be on the level of all; so He eats, drinks, suffers; all this does not affect Him personally but universally."

Meher Baba was asked by one of the group, "Did Christ suffer physically on the cross?" Baba's reply was "If not—why the body? What need for Jesus if he did not suffer? Christ suffered; else what would be the meaning of His taking a body? Through His universal mind, which the knowledge of Godhood continually gives, He experiences that all is nothing and He is sustained by the Godhood's bliss. He suffers but is not affected by the suffering.

"Knowledge means perfect union with God. The Master's suffering is universal suffering, but this universal suffering has no effect on the Master's Godhood.

"How is it then explained when you have become God-realized? No more body, mind, ego, no more universe; only you as God experiencing bliss. You then experience knowledge too, power too; but you do not use power. You are one with this power, this knowledge, this bliss. When you come down for the world, you take universal mind. Now, as God, you see all souls as your own; you see yourself in everything and your universal mind has all minds in one. What every mind suffers comes to your mind. Your mind suffers the suffering of all minds and experiences the happiness of all minds; but as ignorance is in all minds, the suffering is infinitely more than the happiness of these minds. So you suffer infinitely; but your soul, which is fully conscious and enjoys God's bliss continually, which is also infinite, is not affected by this suffering.

"At present, you as soul are unconscious of God and God's bliss. Your mind now suffers or is happy according to your impressions. Soul, as it were, is not affected because through ignorance your soul is identified with your mind, so after knowledge your soul is consciously experiencing God's bliss. Your mind then experiences suffering or happiness but soul is not affected. You are soul. When your mission is complete, then universal mind goes. Universal suffering goes. Then soul enjoys God's bliss."

Where Is God?
(An Interesting Discourse by Meher Baba)
From "Notes from My Diary" by F.H. Dadachanji

One morning during the usual talks with the mandali
Meher Baba lightly touched upon an interesting
subject about God. He abruptly started asking
everyone in the room the question, **"Where is God?"**
All replied on the spur of the moment in various
ways. One said, "Everywhere"; another replied, "In
the soul"; the third, pointing to his heart, softly
whispered, "Here." One argued about the conception
of God and then tried to answer. Another,
expressing his inability for a solution, answered "It is
the eternal problem." Thus the question went around
till it came the turn of Dr. D., who was the last of all
asked by Baba. He seemed to have smilingly surveyed
the situation all the time, and came out with the
spontaneous assertion: "In Meher Baba."

For a moment all were taken aback. It was so
simple, so natural, so easy. Baba then pointed out
that if we all took Him as our Master, Perfect and
One with the Infinite, and honestly believed it, that
was the only conclusion—logical, true and simple.

Meher Baba's object in asking us this question
was probably to draw out of all present what we
have learned in different ways and degrees, and from
that, to explain further. Giving His own answer and
explanation to this most interesting and important
question, Baba went on:

"God is where you [individuals named as K. or A.] are not. That is a reality. Where you [as so and so] are, God is not. That, your being aloof from God, is an illusion. Where your false ego establishes itself as you [so and so] and says you are, God cannot stay. When your false ego as you disappears, God comes in."

Referring to the group's various answers individually given, Baba further explained:

"To say 'God is everywhere' is a general term and nothing new. Pundits all over say that, and Vedanta is full of this explanation. To merely say it is of no use. You must find it, feel it, experience it."

"To say that 'God is in the heart' is again part truth. If God is everywhere, as you all know and say, why then should you limit His being only in the heart and not in the head or your thumb or toe? Why should you try to see Him in one particular part and not in the other? That is a common mistake and characteristic human weakness to spot the highest and most beloved or revered up above, somewhere in the skies or in the heavens; or when sought in the body, to find Him only in the parts men like best, i.e., in the heart or the eye, as if He did not exist equally elsewhere in other parts, in the back or the bones, in the nails or in the flesh. Is God in the rose and not in the thorn? Or in flowers and not in filth? This weakness of seeking God in things you like and shuddering at the idea of His existence in things you do not like or that you abhor, must be overcome. It is only when you rise above all these ideas of good and bad, and recognize, see and feel flowers and filth alike, and find God equally in all, that you could be said to have learned and known something real. Otherwise it is all parrotlike, a false conception, an illusion.

"Besides, taking it for granted that the best and

most ideal abode for God to dwell in the human body is the heart, it must be remembered clearly that, even in this best abode dedicated by human beings for God to dwell, He who is the purest of the pure would not come in unless that abode of the heart, however spontaneously and lovingly offered, is absolutely clear, empty and devoid of any foreign element. The slightest hindrance in the shape of an alien thought would prevent His coming. Those who truly want God to dwell in their hearts must have them utterly clean and empty, devoid of selfish desires, i.e. lust, greed, etc."

Coming to the answer that "one should first form a conception of God and then reply" and the long philosophical explanation that followed, the Master pointed out:

"All these talks are cut and dried. Pundits babble [such things] everywhere, for years, without finding any clue, till they die babbling. The orthodox of all communities listen to these innumerable dissertations by religious students and scriptural scholars, and they form pet beliefs about God and His existence somewhere in the skies or in the best things and not in the others; and they cling to these erroneous ideas tenaciously without the least effort at enlightenment or to go beyond the four walls. They refuse even to talk or listen to the fact of having actual experience and consider it blasphemy even to think of it. It is only these talks and philosophies that appeal to them, and they are quite satisfied with these. That is why I say it is all philosphy and of no use without experience. One must try not only to learn and know, but to feel and experience."

Referring to an answer that "finding God is the eternal problem and struggle," Meher Baba explained:

"It is true; but one must not stop there and make no efforts, taking that problem as impossible to solve and, feeling despondent, give it up. That search and struggle must continue, with added vigor and enthusiasm at every step and the longing developed so intensely that it becomes one's only problem in life. To that end, one should struggle, moving on and on, and try to find all sources of enlightenment in the solution of this.

"The best, easiest and quickest way is to find a Master who has realized God. Although that is not easy at all, and one may have to come across many false and fake ones before he finds the real one; but if the longing for that eternal search is kept up, he will come across one who will guide him right to the goal. Even those living in company with a Master should not feel content and say that they have found everything because they have found a living Master. For even though it is a true statement, it lacks actual experience. And experience can never be had without effort.

"So try, all of you, to see your Master as He really is and not as He appears to you; and even in your Master try to find that infinite experience that pervades everywhere."

Pure Love
An Explanation by Meher Baba

On the eve of December 24, 1939, Meher Baba gave a discourse on "Pure Love" to a visitor, an advocate from the *Mofussil*, who was a simple and plain-spoken man. He quite frankly told Meher Baba that he had heard many people talk about "Love" and still he wondered what Love really was. An interesting conversation ensued, during which Baba explained this subject in His usual simple yet masterly way.

Meher Baba: **"Are you married?"**

Visitor: "Yes."

Meher Baba: **"Have you any children?"**

Visitor: "Yes."

Meher Baba: **"Do you love them?"**

Visitor: "Yes, in the ordinary way. But I cannot say that is Real Love. My object is to have Real Love, not this mayavik affection or attachment. I have visited saints in the hope of experiencing Real Love, but so far have not succeeded in any way."

Meher Baba appreciated the man's longing for True and Divine Love and said: **"You must first understand what Real Love means. Selfish motives, even in what people call love, often deceive them and they mistake selfish feelings for love. I will make the point clear with an example: a person talking of love will say, 'I love my beloved. I want** my beloved to be with me,' and so on. But in all these expressions of love, the 'I' and 'my' are most predominant.

"Another example: suppose you find your child running about in tattered clothes and feeling unhappy about it. You will readily feel for it and do all in your power to get good clothes and make the child happy. On the other hand, if you see a child in the street in similar conditions, i.e., in torn and tattered clothes, would you feel the same and act as readily as you did in the case of your own child? If not, it shows how your attitude towards your own child is merely a result of your selfish feeling.

"Your feelings could be called the outcome of True Love if your attitude towards the unknown child of a stranger in the street were the same as towards your own child under the same conditions.

"**Complete absence of selfishness is therefore the true characteristic and real test of Pure Love.**"

Meher Baba then proceeded to describe how this Pure Love or Divine Love can be experienced. He pointed out that it is not something which could be forced upon a person or snatched away from another person. It is attained after the aspirant has succeeded in overcoming selfishness and when the "I" for him does not exist.

Explaining how this selfless stage could be reached, Meher Baba pointed out: "**It might be said that it is difficult to attain and at the same time it could also be stated that the stage is easy to reach. Paradoxical as these statements might seem, they are nevertheless true.**

"**It is difficult to attain to the stage of selflessness so long as the aspirant has not resolved to reach it. In the absence of a firm determination, the external attachments connected with the lower self prove too strong to be overcome, with the result**

Meher Baba at Happy Valley, 1937.

that the aspirant does not find it possible for him to attain to his goal.

"On the other hand, if the aspirant with a strong will decides once and for all to achieve his aim at any cost, he finds his task easy.

"For example, you have an old coat which you like very much. You cannot get rid of it until you make up your mind and boldly take it off, to do away with it once and for all. The bold decision makes the task easy which would otherwise be difficult."

Meher Baba went on to explain: "Self-renunciation is so necessary for experiencing Pure Love. This 'renunciation' does not mean that one has to leave all the worldly connections and affairs and go to the jungles. It really means remaining in the world and discharging one's own duties faithfully, yet keeping aloof from all attachment. This is not an unattainable ideal, but a practical goal which can be attained with ease, provided of course the aspirant sincerely and boldly resolves to reach it."

Concluding the discourse, Meher Baba pointed out: "Just as a man, when he is hungry, longs for food, similarly when an aspirant desires to experience Pure Love he feels the longing for it, and at the proper time he gets the necessary directions and help from a Master to attain to the goal of desirelessness and is able to enjoy finally the bliss of Divine Love.

"This is a state to be experienced and not to be intellectually described."

SAYINGS
OF MEHER BABA

It is one and the same Universal Being—God—
who plays the different roles of stone, metal,
vegetable, dumb animal and human being; and
through the existence of each of these He
experiences His own gross and subtle
manifestations. It is the same indivisible Being who,
through the existence of a Realized or spiritually
perfect person, experiences His own Real State
which is beyond the gross and subtle planes.

Three curtains—the gross, the subtle, and the
mind—intervene between man and the real truth or
Paramatman. When you remove the subtle curtain
you act through the mind alone; when you are free
of the mind curtain you become one with the
Paramatman.

It is only when you rise above the mind sphere
that you can realize the nothingness of the gross
world. Those who say that God is real and the world
is also real are ignorant. It is because they have very
hazy notions about the Divine realm that they say
that the world is real.

All those who experience the gross world as
real are asleep. Only those who experience it as
unreal can realize God and become awakened.

It is only in the supra-conscious state that the mind is conscious of the real Self.

The act of worship should spring from the heart. Let it be borne in mind that worship from the heart presupposes great efforts. It cannot be evoked by a mere wish. If one decides upon practicing true Bhakti, one has to make heroic efforts in order to achieve fixity of mind, for contrary thoughts are very likely to disturb one's mind.

You have within your Self—the Paramatman— the planes, the planets and the entire universe, but you do not know it. They are within you; but you do not see them there because you see only without and not the real Self within.

In order to enter upon the divine path it is necessary to purify the mind, to abstain entirely from carnal pleasures or sense enjoyments, and to love truth. He is a real aspirant who escapes the snares of Maya, speaks the truth, holds by the truth, and seeks truth only.

Just as darkness becomes invisible in sunlight, so to those who are in the darkness of Maya, God, who is present in all places and at all times, is still invisible.

Intellectual disputations about God will not bring you any nearer to Him and may take you farther away. But persistent heartfelt prayers to Him will lower the veil that now envelops you in darkness.

The existence of almost all persons is under the control of the mind; but scarcely one out of ten thousand persons controls the mind and thus masters the very existence itself.

Happiness and misery, virtue and vice, pleasure and pain, heaven and hell, birth and death are the creations of the mind and depend on the mind.

Many young persons today think that they are wise when they are only proud, and clever when they are only self-conscious.

He who has completely brought the mind under control is a true yogi.

The chief props and agents of Maya are kama, krodh and lobh (lust, anger and greed.) Unless and until you subjugate them it is impossible for you to enter the path that leads to union with God.

Do not try to find excuses or extenuating circumstances for your misdeeds. Unless you repent of your wickedness you cannot improve. To attempt to justify your misdeeds is to smother your conscience and to make virtues out of vices.

The only real renunciation is that which abandons even in the midst of worldly duties all selfish thoughts and desires.

It is praiseworthy to be a genuine sanyasin (spiritual pilgrim) but honest householders are far better than hypocritical sadhus.

Do not be angry with him who backbites you but be pleased; for thereby he serves you by diminishing the load of your sanskaras; also pity him because he increases his own load of sanskaras.

The supreme soul—Paramatman, God—is nowhere to be searched for. For He is very near you; He is with you. Seek Him within. You could easily see Him were it not for the big 'devils' that stand in your way. They are egoism, lust, anger and greed.

Although the one sun, God, who is without a second, shines at all times without a moment's break on all forms, animate as well as inanimate, you are unable to see Him even for a moment, because you are imprisoned in a cell of ignorance coated with desires.

You yourself are the cause of your separation from the Beloved. Annihilate that which is called self and you will thereby gain union with Him.